The Share Economy

T H E

S·H·A·R·E
Economy

CONQUERING STAGFLATION

Martin L. Weitzman

HARVARD UNIVERSITY PRESS
Cambridge, Massachusetts
and London, England
1984

This book is printed on acid-free paper,
and its binding materials have been chosen
for strength and durability.

Library of Congress Cataloging in Publication Data

Weitzman, Martin L., 1942 –
The share economy.

Bibliography: p.
Includes index.
1. Unemployment. 2. Business cycles.
3. Profit-sharing. I. Title
HD5710.W45 1984 339.5 84-665
ISBN 0-674-80582-8 (alk. paper)

Designed by Gwen Frankfeldt

Preface

BECAUSE I BELIEVE THE message of this book is important, I have endeavored to make it accessible to a wide audience. We do not have to live with stagflation if we do not want to. The essential idea of the book — the share economy is a robust natural enemy of unemployment and inflation — is actually quite simple. My intention is that a motivated reader with some background in elementary economics should be able to understand the basic principle of the share economy, and even some of the fine points. For the trained economist in a hurry, chapters 7 through 9 contain the gist of what is original, the central theme being that any compensation system possesses significant macroeconomic externalities. I like to think, however, that there are pertinent novelties of interpretation, exposition, and emphasis sprinkled throughout the book that are also of professional interest. The subject of economics, especially macroeconomics, is currently in a state of disarray and controversy to a degree that the profession has not witnessed for a long time. Far from trying to smooth over these turbulent waters, I hope in passing to convey some flavor of the excitement—and vitality—of political economy today. I also wish to affirm, by example, the central relevance of down-to-earth economic theory for dealing with crucial issues.

Several colleagues kindly gave me detailed comments on an earlier version. I am especially grateful to James S. Earley, Evsey D. Domar, Jon Cohen, James E. Meade, Tibor Scitovsky, John Roemer, Lester C. Thurow, Mervyn King, Carl Lundgren, Tsuneo Ishikawa, and Staffan Burenstam-Linder. Their views, of course, need not coincide with my own.

Excellent assistance was provided by MIT graduate students Michael Kuelwein, Eduardo Borenstein, Christine Roemer, and Mark Bils. The research was aided by a grant from the National Science Foundation.

At Harvard University Press I have been blessed with the editorial skills of Michael Aronson and Joyce Backman, who worked with me as an effective team to improve the manuscript.

To my family I am grateful for tolerating the long nights and disrupted days which this effort entailed. I hope that my activist wife Dorothy approves the message of the book and that my daughter Rodica is placated by seeing her name in print.

Contents

1

There Is a Better Way

THE MARKET ECONOMIES
have long been racked by serious episodes of persistent
unemployment and slow growth. Following Keynes, governments learned to combat depressions through expansionary monetary and fiscal policies. Although this approach was reasonably successful after World War II, especially in the earlier decades 1945–1965, throughout the last two decades unemployment and inflation have become more and more tightly intertwined. Periods of high joblessness and periods of high inflation now alternate, and both frequently occur simultaneously.

The reasons for this worsening economic performance are not yet fully understood. But ironically they may have something to do with the very expectation that Keynesian policies and other humane measures will be used to help unemployed people and bankrupt businesses in a faltering economy. The nasty combination of prolonged stagnation and inflation has been given an equally unpleasant name: stagflation.[1]

"Stagflation is an especially difficult disease to cure because the macroeconomic treatment for one symptom of the malady aggravates the other." The basic way to lower unemployment and speed growth is to stimulate the economy by expansionary fiscal and monetary policy. But the heating-up process seems to accelerate an inflationary momentum that becomes difficult to choke off. And, unfortunately, the basic course of treatment for inflation is to cool down the economy by contractionary policies that cause mass unemployment, slow growth, low productivity, budget deficits, debt crises, and trade imbalances. The result is a "political business cycle" in which countries with mixed economies tend to lurch back and forth from one policy extreme to the other, polarizing the electorate and preventing society from dealing effectively with its underlying real problems. By any reckoning, the direct and indirect costs of stagflation are immense. It seems clear by now that we need new approaches and that the economic system itself is due for a fundamental overhaul.

The thesis of this book is simple. A basic change in employee-compensation arrangements is required to assure that reasonable price stability is compatible with reasonably full employment. So long as we persist in restricting policy options to the usual measures of aggregate fiscal and monetary policy, we will not be able to conquer stagflation. That task is well beyond the range of conventional tools of macroeconomic management.

The principal economic problems of our day have at their

core not *macro* but profoundly *micro* behaviors, institutions, and policies. The war against stagflation cannot be won at the lofty antiseptic plane of pure macroeconomic management. Instead, it must be fought out in the muddy trenches of fundamental micropolitical reform. What is most desperately needed is an improved framework of incentives to induce better output, employment, and pricing decisions at the level of the firm.

Stagflation is not inherent in laissez-faire private enterprise per se. Rather, it is caused by one particular way of paying labor: namely, the compensation of a firm's employees is tied to an outside unit of account (typically money, or perhaps a cost-of-living index) whose value is independent of the firm's well being and of anything the firm does or can do. Stagflation is an unfortunate consequence of the wage-payment system that may sometimes be temporarily offset by good luck or by judicious macroeconomic policy, but eventually necessitates basic reform of the economic mechanism.

The lasting solution to stagflation requires going inside the workings of a modern capitalist economy and correcting the underlying structural flaw directly at the level of the individual firm by changing the nature of labor remuneration. An alternative payment system where it is considered perfectly normal for a worker's pay to be tied to an appropriate index of the firm's performance, say a share of its revenues or profits, puts in place exactly the right incentives automatically to resist unemployment and inflation. Furthermore, it is high time we introduced just such a "natural enemy" and went right after stagflation instead of beating around the bush with clumsy, unreliable macroeconomic instruments whose scope is limited, at best, to shifting between symptoms.

4
The Share Economy

The nature of the required wage reform is not terribly complicated. Essentially the issue is to turn a wage system (which has the underlying attribute of few or no job vacancies at any time) into a share system (having the basic property that there always exists a significant number of unfilled job vacancies). These two systems possess fundamentally different dynamic characteristics. The principal secret for fighting stagflation lies in taking advantage of the vastly superior natural macroeconomic properties of a share system.

To focus the reader's attention, at some risk of oversimplification, let me at once give a concrete if highly idealized example of what I have in mind.

Suppose that wages plus fringe benefits of the average General Motors automobile worker come to $24 per hour. This means that the cost to GM of hiring one additional hour of labor is $24. The extra hour of labor is used to produce more automobiles, which are then sold to yield increased revenue. If the increased revenue exceeds the increased cost, more workers will be hired; in the opposite case, workers will be laid off. Since GM is trying to maximize profits, it will take on (or lay off) workers to the point where the *additional* revenue created by the extra hour of labor is neither more nor less than the additional cost, in this case $24. (The *average* revenue per hour of labor will naturally be higher, say $36, to cover overhead, capital, profits, and the like.)

So far the story is standard. Now imagine that the United Automobile Workers Union decides to try for a somewhat unorthodox labor contract. Instead of having each employed worker receive a wage of $24 per hour, the UAW and GM agree that each of the (say) 500,000 employees will receive as compensation a two-thirds share of GM's aver-

There Is a Better Way

age revenue per worker. In effect, the UAW is allowing GM's revenue pie to be sliced into two pieces, a two-thirds piece going to labor and a one-third piece to management. (In this example, GM's revenue pie is $18 million per hour ($36 × 500,000), while the total share going to labor is $12 million per hour ($24 × 500,000 or 2/3 × $18 million).) At first glance there seems to be no difference: in both cases the employed worker is compensated $24 per hour while management receives $12 per worker-hour to cover other costs and obligations.

But how does GM see things now? Under the old contract, the company had no incentive to expand employment because the cost of an extra worker equaled the additional revenue that worker brought in: $24 per hour. Under the new contract, if GM hires an extra worker its total revenue pie goes up as before by $24 per hour (from $18 million to $18,000,024), but its total labor cost (the slice going to labor) now increases by only two-thirds of $24, or $16 per hour (from $12 million to $12,000,016 = 2/3 × $18,000,024). If the company can find an extra worker to hire, it now stands to clear a profit of $8 per hour. (This comes about because the hourly pay of each of the 500,001 GM employees declines by $8/500,001, from $24 to $23.99998.) Under the new contract GM has an incentive to resist layoffs and, with available unemployed labor, to expand production. As production is expanded, GM automobile prices must come down because more Chevrolets can be sold only if their price is lowered relative to Fords, Toyotas, and the rest.

Next suppose that not only GM but all of the Fortune 500 companies go onto the new contract system. Now as each firm expands, its new workers spend their wages on the products of other firms, creating new demand for autos, enlarging the size of GM's revenue pie, increasing each GM worker's remuneration back up to $24 per hour (or even above $24, since revenues typically expand faster than employment in a recovery) and encouraging further economic expansion.

The expansion ends when every qualified person in the economy seeking work has a job. In each industry the invisible hand of competition and the visible hand of collective bargaining determine compensation and employment levels, just as they have always been determined. The only difference is that now there is full employment, and labor and management are negotiating about the "sharing ratio" (2/3 in the example) instead of the money wage ($24). The average worker, as well as the economy as a whole, is better off under a revenue-sharing system because of its built-in bias toward eliminating unemployment, expanding output, and lowering prices.

Back in our world, follow that new Chevrolet as it rolls off the Detroit assembly line toward its destination in a Philadelphia dealer's parking lot. The GM dealership itself is housed in a simple one-story building internally bisected by a cinderblock wall. The front part of the building is the customer showroom. On the other side of the wall, in the back of the building, is the service department. They are connected by a single unobtrusive wooden or metal door, rarely used. Most of the traffic goes through the large inviting glass doors of the customer showroom and of the service department waiting room which directly, and separately, connect each of them to the outside world.

If not an aesthetic masterpiece, the customer showroom is at least clean and pleasant. It is well lighted, with large picture windows and nice drapes. The walls are freshly

There Is a Better Way

painted. Temperatures are comfortably maintained year round by a good heating and air-conditioning system. Carpets and plush armchairs are strategically placed in areas where the conversation might turn to talk of a purchase. Perhaps there is free coffee and doughnuts. We are so accustomed to this sort of physical environment that we hardly take notice of it or think twice about the effort required to maintain it. Even the washrooms are scrubbed clean.

The customer is well treated by the salesperson, with prompt, courteous service given in an almost ingratiating manner. If the buyer's financial situation is a relevant consideration, the salesperson is understanding and really tries to help by putting together a sufficiently flexible time payment plan to meet the appropriate constraints. An entire organization, euphemistically designated the "General Motors Acceptance Corporation," has been especially created to aid the customer in such matters. Then there is the product itself. The automobiles are available in a wide variety of models and colors, with a great many special options. The salesperson appears to be genuinely interested in explaining the options and helping buyers to choose just what they want. There are so many different combinations that it seems overwhelming at times, even with the assistance of that beautifully illustrated glossy brochure. Certainly the General Motors Corporation has gone out of its way to anticipate what its customers might want and to help them take prompt delivery of a fine product that is well suited to their particular needs and desires.

Now pass through the inconspicuous, infrequently used door that directly connects the customer showroom with the service department. The first thing to notice is that the two sides of the separating wall look quite different. The showroom side was clean and freshly painted. The back side is so dirty that it's unclear when it was last painted. All the working areas of the service department look filthy; obviously no one places much priority on keeping the place clean at all. There are a couple of small windows whose cracked panes of glass are opaque with accumulated dust. Bare lightbulbs provide glaring illumination in what is generally a dim environment with pockets of semidarkness everywhere. This part of the building has no air conditioning and the heating doesn't function very well — so it is hot in the summer and cold in the winter. The service department washroom is grimy and unkept.

Human relations are fair here, but the employer clearly does not go out of his way to please the employee — if anything it is the other way round. There is no thought about how to make the work more interesting or better suited to the employee's wants. Hiring and firing decisions are made almost exclusively on the basis of narrow economic considerations. The special financial need of an employee or the idea of using more flexible time payment plans (such as the possibility of employees' borrowing money) never even enters the employer's mind.

The artificial cinderblock wall does more than physically divide the dealership building. It separates two different worlds of human relations. The automobile dealer acts as if he really cares about his customers. But he doesn't seem to care at all about his workers.

The essence of the contrast is epitomized by the following thought experiment. Suppose a man, who happens to be a qualified mechanic, enters the front of the dealership building intending to purchase an automobile. In all likelihood he will be eagerly sold as many cars as he wants to buy

There Is a Better Way

at the going price. But if that same man goes to the back of the building — or to the GM plant — seeking a job at the current wage, chances are he will be turned down.

The difference between the treatment of consumers and workers is not accidental. Although naturally modified by circumstances of time and place, the observation that consumers are more highly favored than workers reflects a deeply ingrained pattern characteristic of advanced capitalist countries (with the conceivable exception of Japan). That this is hardly a feature of all economic systems is immediately demonstrated by the example of socialist countries, where the pattern is reversed: there consumers are less gratified than workers.

A strong economic determinism underlies this striking asymmetry of relations in the capitalist system. And, as will be shown, it is very much connected to the form of labor payment. Just as a wage system exhibits weak resistance to unemployment and inflation in the economy at large, so it demonstrates a pronounced discrepancy between the treatment of workers and of consumers on the microeconomic level. In contrast, the share macroeconomy exhibits strong natural tendencies toward full employment and price stability, while its microeconomic counterpart turns out to be a firm whose managers lavish as much attention on pleasing their workers as on satisfying their customers.

These are strong claims that at this stage must sound strange or even astounding. How can it possibly be that a mere change in the formula by which labor is paid can have such profound economic and social consequences?

2
Three Major Decisions
of the Firm

TO UNDERSTAND WHAT STAG-
flation is really about and why wage reform is likely to be a
crucial component of any genuine solution, it is useful to
comprehend more fully how a market economy works —
and sometimes doesn't work. The first step in that direction
is to cut in at the micro level and analyze the way a firm
makes three major economic decisions: (1) how much output to produce; (2) how much labor to hire; (3) what price to
charge.

Because all important economic actions originate here,
the firm is the vital unit of an economy. Actually, the firm *is*
the economy in a microcosm. So anyone who wants to comprehend the functioning of an economic system should

begin with a thorough understanding of how a typical firm operates.[1]

At the center of modern industrial capitalism is a relatively small number of large-scale firms that set the tone for the entire system. I have in mind such companies as the Fortune 500, a group that accounts for over 80 percent of sales in the industrial sector. If these big corporations are doing well, so is the economy, and vice versa. Neither pure monopolists nor perfect competitors, these "competitive monopolists" or "monopolistic competitors" cover the product spectrum with a shingle-like pattern of overlapping market areas within which they compete vigorously for customers.

For a variety of reasons, including dynamic learning effects, modern mass-production methods tend to be characterized by economies of scale or average costs that decline as output is expanded over the long run. In most industries the cost per unit of output is less for a high-volume producer than for a low-volume producer. From automobiles to books to computers—and on through the product alphabet—every business person knows that unit costs typically go down with the size of the production run.

The propensity for unit costs to decline with volume creates a strong tendency toward concentration of ever bigger firms producing larger outputs. Counteracting this tendency toward bigness is the fact that not all people want exactly the same thing—some may prefer one firm's particular product, while others like what is offered by a rival firm. You may like the peppiness of a Ford Mustang while I want the service reliability of a Toyota Corolla. A Maytag washing machine is initially more expensive to buy than a Whirlpool, but it saves on future energy and maintenance costs. The IBM computer is better for business uses, but the

Digital is superior for scientific work. Such examples can be replicated almost indefinitely.

Products are differentiated either artificially (by the manufacturer), or naturally, or both. Spatial distance and transportation costs alone provide a powerful impetus toward natural differentiation into overlapping regional markets. And the ingenuity of capitalist firms in contriving to make semiartificial differences in toothpastes, soaps, pain relievers, beer, or breakfast cereals is surely too well known to require elaboration. The result of this proliferation of competing near-substitutes is that any one producer faces a limited market for his particular differentiated product. The predisposition for declining costs to cause high-volume production is thus offset by constrained buyer interest. As Adam Smith succinctly expressed the thought over two centuries ago: "The division of labor" [now called increasing returns to scale] "is limited by the extent of the market."

The way in which a firm perceives the extent of its market is through the demand it encounters. Every firm knows that demand is a function of (among other things) price — that is, there is an indirect relation between the price a firm chooses to charge and the number of sales it can make. If Ford is offering automobile rebates, it will attract more customers and the volume of sales will increase directly with the size of rebate offered. The lower the price of Digital's personal computer, the more computers Digital will sell by bringing totally new customers into the home market and also by cutting into the established markets of Apple and IBM. When Budweiser is "on sale," more cases of it get sold relative to other beers.

The most significant characteristic of a demand function, and a concept that crops up just about everywhere in economics, is its *elasticity*. As the name implies, elasticity is a measure of the sensitivity or responsiveness of demand to changes in price. The elasticity of demand is the percentage increase in the number of items sold that would be induced by a 1 percent decrease in the price. If demand is relatively inelastic, it means that by lowering its price the firm gains comparatively few new buyers, while raising its price does not much discourage its old customers. Common sense tells us, and theory confirms, that if the firm faces a relatively inelastic demand for its product, it tends to charge a comparatively high price and hold back output. On the other hand, relatively elastic demand means that lowering the price will bring in lots of new buyers to the firm, while raising the price will drive away many old customers. In this case our common sense dictates, and theory verifies, that the firm is not going to mark its price up much above cost of production.

There is a theoretical bound on how inelastic a firm's demand can be. Taking all things into account (including reactions of rival firms), the long-run elasticity of demand faced by a monopolistic competitor must always be greater than one. Otherwise it would be profitable to raise price by 1 percent and lower sales by less than 1 percent — thereby increasing revenues *and* lowering production costs. So the actual elasticity of demand for a firm's product must lie in a range from one (relatively inelastic) to infinity (relatively elastic). The limiting case of infinitely elastic demand is called perfect competition. It means that if the firm raises its price a tiny bit it loses all its customers, whereas if it lowers its price a little it gains more buyers than it can handle. Under perfect competition the firm has a very limited ability to choose its price and is, in effect, a price taker.

The dependence of each firm's sales upon the price it

charges can also be expressed the other way around. Given any target volume of sales the firm wishes to market, there is a unique price it can charge just to clear that volume. In other words, if quantity depends upon price we can just as easily think in terms of the inverse relation, where price depends upon quantity.

Going one step further, we can multiply price times quantity to obtain *total revenue* as a function of the target volume of sales. For each volume of output it wants to sell, the total-revenue function tells the firm what revenues it can hope to receive after charging the particular price necessary to clear that volume of output. The idea that revenue can be ultimately viewed as a function of quantity sold is crucial in helping the firm to plan a sensible output and pricing strategy.

Suppose the firm was producing and marketing some particular volume of output and receiving a corresponding total revenue. Suppose now the firm plans to increase the volume of output by one unit. To market the new volume (old volume plus one), it must lower its price slightly, which results in a new total revenue (the new volume of output times the new price). *Marginal revenue* is the difference between the new and old revenues. In other words, marginal revenue is the extra or additional revenue obtained after a planned unit increase in sales, taking account of the inevitable lowering of price required to expand market volume by one unit.

Here is a concrete example. Suppose the price of a Ford Escort is $7,500 and 200,000 units are sold per year, yielding annual revenues of $1.5 billion. Let the long-run elasticity of demand for a Ford Escort be 3. (Demand for consumer durables tends to be quite elastic; in this example prospective buyers can switch to or from Chevrolet Chevettes,

Three Major Decisions of the Firm

Toyota Corollas, Dodge Omnis, and a host of other substitutes. Throughout this book a demand elasticity of 3 is chosen only because it is convenient for illustrative purposes — nothing substantive would be altered in the analysis if a different elasticity were assumed, although specific numerical results would naturally change.) Were Ford to lower its price by 1 percent, from $7,500 to $7,425, it could sell an additional 6,000 Escorts per year (3 percent of 200,000). That would yield annual revenues of $1.53 billion ($206,000 \times \$7,425$), an increase of $30 million per year. The marginal revenue of *one* extra Ford Escort is therefore $5,000 ($30 million $\div$ 6,000 Escorts).

The fact that marginal revenue turns out to be less than price in the example is no coincidence. If one extra Ford Escort could be sold each year without depressing the market clearing price of $7,500, the marginal revenue would exactly equal the price: $7,500. But to induce buyers to take just one more Escort per year requires that the price be lowered by a tiny amount: 1.25¢ to be exact. Now a price reduction of that magnitude may not seem like much, but when you are selling 200,000 units per year, it adds up to $2,500. That 200,001st Escort being sold brings in $7,449.9875 (or $7,449.99 rounded off to the nearest penny), but it is spoiling the market for the other 200,000 Escorts by $2,500; so its *marginal* contribution to revenue is $5,000 ($7,500 − $2,500).

There is another way of making the point that marginal revenue is less than price. The average revenue (total revenue per unit sold) is just the price, and it naturally declines as output rises. There is no way that average revenue can decline with the volume of output unless marginal revenue is *less* than average revenue. Only if the last increment of revenue is less than the average of all preceding increments will the average be pulled down when output increases by one unit. (A baseball player's batting average declines after a game if and only if he bats lower during the game than his season's average before the game.)

The ratio of average revenue (or price) to marginal revenue is an important number characterizing the demand relation which, for reasons that will later become clear, I call the *markup coefficient*. The markup coefficient is closely related to the elasticity of demand. (Although only the nature of the general relationship between them is important, rather than the exact formula, it turns out that the markup coefficient equals the ratio of *elasticity* to *elasticity minus one*. Thus, the Ford Escort in the example has a markup coefficient of 1.5.)

Firms facing elastic or price-responsive demand have a low markup coefficient; when the price does not have to be lowered very much to sell more output, the marginal revenue brought in by an extra unit is not much below its price. The limiting case here is perfect competition, which means that demand is infinitely elastic or the firm can essentially sell as much as it wants at the going price. In this extreme case price *equals* marginal revenue so that the markup coefficient is one. On the other hand, firms with relatively inelastic (or price-unresponsive) demand will possess a high markup coefficient. In this case a higher volume of sales can only be achieved by significantly lowering the price or "spoiling the market," resulting in a high ratio of average to marginal revenue.

The demand or revenue side is one half of the picture of the firm. The other half is provided by the supply or cost side. When put together, the two compose a complete theoretical representation.

A firm cannot directly control its sales. That depends on

its customers. Instead, given any state of the market, a firm can indirectly control sales through the price it charges. But to be consistent, the sales on the demand side must match the production on the supply side. (Slight differences are allowed by inventory changes, which must be corrected later.)

Total cost of production is a function of the volume of output. As was already noted, average cost tends to decline with higher output, in part because fixed overhead (or what firms sometimes call indirect cost) is spread out over a larger quantity. Marginal cost is, of course, the additional cost of producing one extra unit of output, and it usually does not show any pronounced tendency to vary with output, at least over a broad range up to full capacity. Empirical studies show that marginal cost (or what firms more usually call direct production cost) is relatively constant over wide variations in capacity utilization for most industrial products and services.

Now the elements are in place for determining how a firm plans its three big economic decisions:

(1) output is selected at the level where marginal revenue equals marginal cost;

(2) as much labor is hired as is needed to produce that output;

(3) price is set by multiplying marginal cost times the markup coefficient.

Why are these rules the relevant description of how the firm operates? Because only when the firm solves its major decisions by these criteria will it be maximizing profits.

Profit is the difference between the revenue a firm receives and the cost it must pay out. When profits are maximized, it must mean that the extra revenue from selling an additional unit of output is exactly offset by the extra cost of production. If marginal revenue exceeds marginal cost, the firm can increase profits by expanding production. On the other hand, when marginal revenue is less than marginal cost, the firm can save more from cost reduction by cutting back production than it loses in forgone revenue. The idea that the firm establishes its output level at the point where marginal revenue equals marginal cost is a fundamental principle (it may even be *the* fundamental principle) of microeconomics.

Once it has been decided how much to produce, in effect it has also been decided how many workers to hire, given the unique relation between output and labor. A reason the hiring of labor has been singled out as one of the three major economic decisions of the firm worthy of separate emphasis is that, in the aggregate, labor costs constitute 80 percent of national income outlays on factors of production. (The returns to capital and land constitute the other 20 percent.) Besides, this book is largely about the determination of employment levels. From that perspective, the labor-hiring decision is arguably the most important of the big three.

The ratio of average revenue to marginal revenue is a number characterizing the demand relation I called the markup coefficient. Since average revenue equals price and since marginal revenue equals marginal cost in a profit-maximizing state, the profit-maximizing ratio of price to marginal cost is also given by the markup coefficient. This means that the firm follows the simple pricing rule of marking up its marginal production cost by a numerical factor (which essentially depends upon the elasticity of demand), hence the term "markup coefficient."

So, through the markup coefficient, price depends upon cost (especially labor cost). If the firm faces a very elastic demand, the equilibrium price will not be marked up very much above the cost of producing an extra unit. If, on the other hand, the firm faces an inelastic demand, it then possesses a significant degree of monopoly power and will mark up its price considerably above marginal cost of production.

The fact that the monopolistically competitive firm always charges a price for what it sells *higher* than the marginal cost of producing it (and thereby restrains output to keep the price there) has significant implications for the functioning of a market economy. The firm with some degree of control over its price never exists in a state of neutral equilibrium where supply equals demand. Always, in good times and in bad, the monopolistically competitive firm wishes to supply *more* at the going price than its customers are willing to take because the price exceeds marginal production cost.

Suppose an impartial observer from another world picked at random a nonagricultural good or service and its price from our economy. To his question, "Do you want to buy more at that price?" the potential customers would answer no. If the impartial observer posed the question, "Do you want to sell more at that price?" to the seller, the answer would be yes. Supply equals demand only in the rare case of perfect competition where the markup coefficient is exactly one, price equals marginal cost, and the firm does not have to worry about spoiling its market.

The discussion has so far been carried out as if the firm's environment were stable and well known. In reality, every firm is adrift in a sea of uncertainty. What we ask of a good theory of the firm in such circumstances is not that it be precise; that is too much to ask of any economic theory. Rather, the good theory should be a reasonable description of general tendencies whenever the background uncertainty is like random noise — adding a bit here, subtracting a little there, yet without discernible trend or direction. But what should the firm do when it becomes obvious that the uncertainty is not like background static, and instead something fundamental has changed which was not envisioned and is not likely to be reversed soon?

This book is concerned with responses to unanticipated economic change. So it is important to understand how the three major decisions of the monopolistically competitive firm are affected by a changed environment. How, for instance, does the firm react to a decline in demand for its product? Such a decline might be caused by a shift in tastes, the entry of a rival firm, or, most likely of all, a general recession.

When demand declines, it means that the firm cannot sell as much as before. There is still a pervasive inverse relationship between price and quantity demanded that is similar to what existed before; it is simply that now the relationship has everywhere deteriorated so that, at *any* given price, less can be sold than before. Provided that demand has uniformly declined by the same percentage at every price (which seems to be a decent empirical approximation), it can be shown that both the price elasticity of demand and the markup coefficient will not be changed. If, in addition, marginal cost is roughly constant in some range (which is also a reasonably good approximation when wages are unchanged), then an important inference can be drawn.

Because the markup coefficient is nearly fixed and because marginal cost is approximately constant, the profit-maximizing reaction to a change in demand is overwhelmingly a quantity response, with price remaining practically unchanged. So long as wage costs are stable, whenever product demand is depressed the firm will react principally by cutting back production and laying off workers, but leaving its price intact. Though this rule is subject to many modifications, it nevertheless stands out as an important generalization. The primary adjustment of a capitalist system to demand fluctuations is on the side of quantities rather than prices. Once granted that wages are rigid, it is not mysterious why prices should also be rigid. Ford can physically cut its sticker prices as soon as a new car rolls off the assembly line, put in place a customer rebate program within forty-eight hours (twenty-four if its dealers have been alerted to stand by for instructions), and instantaneously communicate to its dealerships any changes in the invoice cost basis of the cars they are currently holding. But so long as marginal production costs remain tolerably constant, these ways of responding to a recession are generally less profitable than scaling back output.

As another example of how the profit-maximizing firm reacts to changes, consider what happens if the wage rate, or for that matter the cost of raw materials used in fixed proportions with labor, goes up. Then the cost increase is passed on into a higher price through the markup coefficient. Naturally, sales must be contracted to support the higher price; output declines and workers are laid off. Here is another important empirical generalization: a capitalist economy reacts to cost increases by raising prices and lowering production. The converse proposition is also true. Other things being equal for the firm, a lower wage means higher employment, more output, and lower prices.

The following simple observations will be important to my general thesis. Starting from a profit-maximizing position, if more labor were to be hired:

(1) price would decline (because more labor means more output, which can be sold only if the price is dropped);

(2) revenue per worker would decline (because the marginal revenue created by an additional worker is less than the average revenue per worker);

(3) profit per worker would decline (because total profits, already at a maximum, now have to be spread out over more workers).

Of course, hiring less labor would reverse these conclusions.

There is one further consideration. What has been discussed so far might be called a conditional description. It tells how the major economic decisions of the firm are derived from the profit-maximizing rule "marginal revenue equals marginal cost," given that the firm chooses to operate in the first place. In the long run, a firm will choose to operate (not to shut down) only if it is making some profit —if its total revenue minus its total cost is positive. But when a firm is making a lot of profit, that acts like the scent of blood to a school of hungry sharks. There is strong inducement, in extreme cases bordering on panic, for other firms to squeeze into the market with their own version of a similar product. A very profitable IBM computer business will entice a Digital Equipment Corporation to come in and bite off the small scientific computer segment of the market, or an Apple Company to nibble away at home computers, or a Control Data Corporation to go after the giant computer market, leaving IBM with the lion's share of the (still very lucrative) large business computers.

Capitalism is a dynamic system, constantly renewed by what Joseph Schumpeter called a "perennial gale of creative destruction."[2] Innovative new firms are perpetually bursting upon the scene, making big initial profits and clearing the way for other firms to follow in their wake. Eventually, the imitators and competitors lower the original profit margins. In senescence, the profits of a firm start to decline and finally, unless there is some rejuvenation, death sets in when losses become regular. So my description of the three major economic decisions of the firm is but a still frame from a movie sequence that goes on and on. The movie as a whole carries a more graphic implication; there is perhaps *some* long-run tendency for pure economic profits to drift toward zero.

3
The Coordination Problem of a Market Economy

A WELL-FUNCTIONING market economy is an intricate symphony of production and distribution. Individuals and organizations motivated essentially by self-interest are somehow orchestrated into a master plan as if directed by what Adam Smith called an invisible hand. The matching and coordination problems routinely solved every day by capitalism are of a high order of complexity. That this decentralized system can achieve spectacular material accomplishments has long been recognized and admired even by its critics, among the more imaginative of them Marx, Engels, Lenin, and Mao.

The modern economy owes its high standard of living to its capital equipment and to an extraordinary division of labor. Economies of mass production are impossible without an extensive specialization of roles and functions within the large firm, not unlike the way individual cells are specialized in a multicellular biological organism. As an extreme example, the assembly-line worker may repeat one tedious task hour after hour, day after day, year after year. In the movie classic *Modern Times*, Charlie Chaplin plays a factory hand whose entire job consists of endlessly repeating the same motion with a wrench to tighten the nut on a particular bolt. There is a standard joke about the machine shop whose workers vie with each other for the novelty of being able to lathe-cut an occasional batch of left-handed screws. People have remained generalists in consumption throughout history (though at ever higher levels), but they have increasingly become specialists in production.

With greater specialization comes the reward of higher productivity. But it is contingent upon ever more cooperation and interdependence. The larger the scale of production units in an economy, the more acute the need for coordination. Like their domesticated plants and animals, people have become so specialized in production that they are extremely vulnerable to any breakdown in the existing order. When aggregrate demand is weak, the worker laid off from a division-of-labor team in one factory cannot readily join a team in a different factory. The unemployed urban worker of today who has been separated from his team cannot effectively produce on his own, or in small groups, nor can he easily retreat back into a self-sufficient existence. (During recessions we actually observe rural inhabitants attempting to adjust by switching to such small-scale activities as raising vegetables, digging clams, picking or selling apples, gathering firewood, and the like.) Even if unemployed workers could do any of these things, they would not be at all productive compared to what is socially attainable under large-scale division of labor.

How does the market economy as a whole coordinate itself in a consistent way so that it can fully exploit the division of labor? Why is not too little of this, or too much of that, being produced? With so much interdependence, what prevents a loose string from unraveling the whole ball of twine? After all, turning loose millions of greedy, myopic, uncontrolled individuals and groups each doing their own thing surely *seems* like a prescription for chaos and decay. Obviously there must be some deep-seated self-correcting forces tending toward coordination or the economy would never be where it is today.

We have already seen how the individual firm plans its three major decisions given its demand function and its costs of production. But where do the demand functions come from? And what determines costs (especially labor cost, by far the most important component)? How is the whole system connected in a consistent way?

At the present state of our knowledge, economics can only give answers in terms of long-run tendencies. That is, these kinds of global questions can be definitively answered only when external shocks or changes are sufficiently slow-moving, or happened long enough ago, or occur with sufficient regularity to warrant describing the economy as being in a condition of "equilibrium."

Equilibrium is a fictitious stationary state of the economy where all agents have adjusted to the current situation as best they can. No agent wants to change what he, she, or it is doing given the constraints each faces. Equilibrium is the state toward which an economy drifts if left undisturbed. Unfortunately, the equilibrating mechanism need not be especially quick-acting, and in some actual markets the adjustment process may be exasperatingly slow. Such short-run disequilibrium phenomena as involuntary unemployment in labor markets can last quite a long time.

Probably the best way to think of equilibrium is as a norm or abstraction or point of departure that indicates the tendencies toward which the economy is gravitating, even though it may never quite get there in practice. An economy that has just been subjected to a whopping increase in the price of imported oil, or in which investment spending has dropped precipitously, or where unemployment is massive, is not in a state of long-run equilibrium. But even in those cases it is essential to understand the nature of the equilibrium that the economy is coming from or going toward. Just as a suddenly disoriented person who hasn't yet learned how to adjust to an unexpected shock will cling tenaciously to a few old notions while at the same time being forced to abandon some others, so in its disequilibrium response an economic system tends to hold some variables at or near their old equilibrium values, while allowing others to change much more rapidly.

Any firm is doing two things at once. It is creating value, by producing and distributing a good or a service that people want. And it is simultaneously paying out this value to factors of production in the form of wages, interest, rents, and profits. Because practically every person is a specialist in production and a generalist in consumption, only a very small fraction of the income paid out by a firm is directly returned to it as demand for its own product. Instead, the workers and stockholders of a firm spend their income largely on the products of other firms. So the demand for *this* firm's specific product comes largely out of the factor incomes generated by all the *other* firms in the economy.

An economy is a circle of interdependent relations. Given

the demand for its product, each firm chooses to produce where marginal revenue equals marginal cost, paying out factor incomes accordingly. When the implied factor incomes from all the firms are spent, the resulting demands for each firm's product must exactly match and confirm the demand pattern originally postulated. Otherwise there is a basic inconsistency, and the behavior of the firms will change to accommodate the different set of generated demands. Only when there is complete consistency between the amounts demanded by the factors of production and the profit-maximizing outputs produced by each firm will the economy be in a state of equilibrium.[1] An extraordinary number of consistency conditions must simultaneously be fulfilled. As Friedrich Hayek once expressed the idea, "Every day millions of equations are being solved in the market place."

What about labor and wages? Right from the beginning, the economist confronts in the labor market a blatant contradiction. At a high level of abstraction, labor is by far the most interchangeable commodity in the economy. If you standardize for quality, is not "aggregate labor" a more homogeneous concept than "aggregate minerals" or "aggregate capital"? A coalminer and a fruitpicker are infinitely closer substitutes than the products they handle. Rolled sheet and I-beams, produced by the same steelworker in different mills, are virtually inconvertible in use. At the level of an entire economy, no other commodity comes even close to being as substitutable as labor is across its various roles and functions. On this basis alone there would appear to be a strong *a priori* case that the labor market should be essentially competitive.

On the other hand, few other markets are as loaded down with institutional, social, psychological, and historical trappings as the labor market. Everywhere they look, labor economists can see special features that undermine simple-minded monistic descriptions of what is happening. There are labor unions, collective-bargaining agreements, minimum-wage laws, unemployment insurance, market segmentation, barriers to entry, seniority privileges, envious interpersonal comparisons, varying degrees of job disutility, rent elements, differences in labor quality, noncompeting groups, imperfect mobility, discrimination, incomplete information, training costs, search costs, transactions costs, and a host of other buzzwords that conjure up images of compromising features. To picture the extreme renditions of this sort of description sometimes given by institutionalists is almost to envision a feudal enclave in an otherwise capitalistic economy.

What is one to make of these two contradictory strands? The answer surely depends upon what it is going to be used for. If your aim is to focus in on fine close-up details and you wish to do justice to the facts, you must rely on a heavily institutional approach. But I think the unique long-run substitutability of labor among different uses actually makes the competitive theory a rather good description of *long-run tendencies* in the labor market. If you want to get a big picture of wage determination, the competitive theory is reasonably appropriate as an account of the important and ultimately decisive tendencies in the labor market, even if it cannot be taken as a literal representation of day-to-day events.[2]

John R. Hicks, summarizing his own view as an economic theorist and as a one-time labor economist, concluded in his Commentary to the second edition of *The Theory of Wages*

(1964): "It may, I think, be granted that there are strong reasons why the market in which a firm *sells* should normally be imperfectly competitive (for some individuality in its products is one of the bases on which a firm can maintain its own individuality). There is, however, no such reason why there should be 'monopsony' on the buying side; it may occur, but its occurrence (one would think) would be relatively exceptional . . . Thus it can plausibly be maintained that our standard picture of a firm should be such that it is a price-taker on the side of inputs, but a price-maker on the side of outputs."

In this book I am primarily interested in the general theory of wage determination, and I have little hesitation in describing the labor market as competitive for that purpose. Or at least the labor market behaves "as if" it is competitive, in the sense that countervailing power between buyers and sellers of labor is sufficiently balanced that neither party has a clear upper hand and both possess approximately equal bargaining strength.[3] The economy-wide real wage is not very different from what would be determined by competitive forces in the labor market.

Equilibrium in the labor market means full employment. Almost by definition, there can be no unemployment in equilibrium because that would represent an unsettled state of the economy. When there is unemployed labor, so goes the classical argument, forces will be set in motion to drive down the wage relative to product demands. However slowly they act, such forces will *eventually* succeed in restoring full employment. In this world view, involuntary unemployment is mostly a phenomenon of short-run disequilibrium, although such a "short run" can sometimes last an uncomfortably long time.

In a truly stationary economy, where the equilibrating

Coordination Problem of a Market Economy

tendencies have had sufficient time to work themselves out, all workers will be fully employed. So the only general theory of wage determination we have is very much a theory of how wages are set in a tight labor market. The most we can expect from such a theory is that it will be a decent approximation for an economy not too far removed from full employment. That may actually be enough, because wages have a great deal of inertia. But the theory undoubtedly starts to unravel as a recession becomes prolonged.

What determines the cost of labor or the wage rate in equilibrium? The brief answer, which must be interpreted as a long-run tendency rather than as a literal description, is this: in equilibrium, all workers of a given quality or productivity are paid the "extra value" they produce on the margin for a firm.

When an additional unit of labor is hired, it produces some extra output for the firm. Multiplying that extra output by the marginal revenue the output brings in, and then subtracting the marginal cost of any additional needed materials, determines the marginal value to the firm of the extra worker. In equilibrium, the wage paid by the firm must equal the value that the last, extra unit of labor brings in — or else the firm would expand or contract its employment accordingly. Furthermore, in equilibrium all firms must be paying more or less the *same* wage (corrected for labor quality) — or else the low-paying firms will be systematically losing workers to the high-paying firms, and forces will thereby be set in motion to make the firms equalize wage rates.

If all of this seems rather abstract, such a reaction is appropriate. Labor is a notoriously "different" commodity from bread or steel. There are many, many ways in which the labor market is more complex than has been indicated here. Yet, for all its shortcomings, for all the missing details, the marginal-value theory provides a fairly accurate picture of how the general level of wages is determined in the long run. When all is said and done, the guiding principle in determining wage levels remains the idea that each type of labor is paid a return just equal to its own best-use marginal contribution to the net value of output. It is to this norm or approximation that wages of a market economy tend over time, throughout history and across nations, so long as there is reasonably full employment.

One further point remains to be noted here. In equilibrium, the *way* labor is paid does not matter since all workers will end up receiving the same *amount* anyway (adjusted, as always, for inherited or acquired productivity differences). A straight wage, profit sharing, revenue sharing, or any other system are all the same in equilibrium because long-run forces assure that labor is paid its marginal value to the producer, no matter what the ostensible form of the compensation arrangement. This will come about because the coefficient or parameter of profit share per worker or revenue share per worker, or whatever else is pertinent for a particular compensation system, will adjust over time to compensate each worker the common marginal value of labor. If the going rate for the skill level of an automobile assembler is $24 per hour and GM workers are to be paid some fraction of GM revenues of $36 per hour, the long-run value of the revenue-sharing coefficient or parameter must adjust to two-thirds.

Whether paid a straight wage or a share of profits or revenues, or whatever else, the bottom line to workers is how much money they make. Workers will gravitate toward the higher-paying jobs, and away from the lower-paying jobs, no matter how they are paid. A firm trying to set its compensation too low (whatever the *form* of the compensation) may get away with it for a while, but eventually will get caught. Gradually the firm will observe that its workers are quitting more readily. At the same time, it will be harder to recruit new employees of comparable quality. So the long-run equilibrium tendencies are toward making all firms pay the same dollar remuneration (corrected for individual worker skills), despite the form of the compensation and equal everywhere to the marginal value of labor.

Another way of putting it is that, in the equilibrium state of all compensation systems, the average cost of labor (what labor actually gets paid per unit) is the same for all firms and is everywhere equal to the (common) marginal value of labor. But, as we shall see, only in the wage system are the average and marginal costs of labor the same. In other systems (such as revenue sharing or profit sharing), the marginal cost to the firm of hiring an extra unit of labor is less than the average cost, with important implications for how the labor market then operates.

What is it like to live in the world of a monopolistically competitive economy?

In the first place, the overwhelming majority of its firms set prices above marginal costs of production. When the price of a commodity is above marginal production cost, it means that the firm would like to sell more than it can actually sell at the price it itself has chosen to post. Each monopolistically competitive firm is thus motivated to bring in new buyers and to hold on to old customers, since every extra sale now means some more profit (equal to the difference between price and marginal cost). Under perfect competition — where the firm cannot influence price, demand is infinitely elastic, and the markup coefficient is one — price equals marginal cost, so the firm is essentially indifferent about whether it gains a new customer or loses an old one. (It is difficult to find many examples of perfect competition; agriculture, the prototype, now constitutes less than 5 percent of gross national product in the United States.)

The two world views are diametrically opposed. A perfectly competitive economy (pure agriculture) means anonymous business dealings among buyers and sellers with equilibrium determined where desired demand just equals desired supply. In a monopolistically competitive economy (more like the world we live in), the desired supply of goods exceeds desired demand. Transactions between buyer and seller are strictly constrained by demand at all times. Buyers under monopolistic competition are continually able to purchase as much as they want, while the product market is invariably long on the supply side. At the profit-maximizing price it sets, the monopolistically competitive firm always wants to supply more output. Naturally it doesn't want to spoil its market by expanding *planned* output at the expense of a lower price; but once a posted price is in effect, the monopolistic competitor is eager to increase sales.

Of course the amount sold of any good always equals the amount bought, by definition. But this is very different from saying that supply (the amount sellers want to sell at a given price) equals demand (the amount buyers want to buy at a given price). The "law of supply and demand" is not supposed to be a trivial definition; it is an important statement — about the identity of buyers' and sellers' intentions at the equilibrium price — but one that applies *only* to perfectly competitive markets.

The idea that we live in an economy of goods and services where "demand equals supply" even as an abstraction represents a deeply erroneous perception of what political economy has taught us. In fact we live in a world where the normal condition of the product market is that supply exceeds demand, which is a very different paradigm indeed! To overlook this essential aspect is to miss a great deal of what capitalism is all about. Too many economists seem unmindful of the basic point that producers *set* prices, in systematic relation to costs, so that supply exceeds demand in 95 percent of the product markets of advanced capitalist countries. This oversight results in quite a bit of misleading, and sometimes downright wrong, theorizing about a great many important issues in both micro- and macroeconomics.

As an economic system, monopolistic competition exerts steady pressure on output markets, in good times and bad, because at any given moment firms are actively seeking to expand production and sales. Our very way of life is shaped by this asymmetric bias.[4]

We live, all of us denizens of a market economy, in a buyer's paradise. As consumers we are actively courted by the hidden persuaders of advertising; our opinions about what we like to consume are eagerly sought out and listened to; completely new products and new variations of old products are continually created to gratify our existing wants and to anticipate our future desires; sellers trip over themselves in an effort to improve in our eyes the image of their product and the quality of the services accompanying its sale and maintenance. These and other forms of non-price competition can be taken to undesirable extremes, but they do account for a substantial part of the richness, dynamism, diversity, and, yes, quality of economic life under capitalism. Little of this, it is important to realize, stems from universal natural law or human nature. Rather, these features reflect the unintended consequences of a particular market structure that happens to be rather widespread.

The predominance of product markets where price exceeds marginal cost also has important sociological implications. As just one example, take the following simple observation. Our colleges and business schools offer innumerable courses on marketing techniques but almost none on buying techniques. Why? Because anyone with money can pretty easily figure out what to buy, whereas it takes a real knack to know how to sell things. A good salesperson is far more highly valued and rewarded in the business world than a good commercial buyer. (It is the purchasing agent, however, who gets the presents at Christmas time, whereas the salesperson has the expense account for entertaining potential buyers.) Product advertising is everywhere. As a civilization, we spend a vastly greater amount of resources on selling than on buying. Our folklore and literature reflect this. From the informal traveling-salesman stories and the *New Yorker* cartoons about life on Madison Avenue to serious work like Arthur Miller's *Death of a Salesman*, we are a culture of persistent sellers trying to overcome the sales resistance of coy buyers. Rebates, bonuses, and ingratiating behavior, not to mention bribes, favors, and kickbacks, are invariably given by sellers to buyers, not the other way around.

To know the sociology of economic life in the Soviet Union and other socialist countries is to confront an antiworld to this one. There, where goods are scarce and the marginal value to a buyer is often far higher than the price, everything is reversed. (We see occasional glimpses of this same pattern reversal here whenever price controls are used to repress demand; but nothing in our past or present can match the richness of everyday Soviet experience in such matters.) If under capitalism the merchant's best wares are on display up front, then under socialism they are hidden in the back storeroom — where the real business transactions often take place. The *tolkach* ("pusher") of the Soviet state enterprise — the crafty, highly valued, and well-paid commercial agent — is actually a skilled buyer who knows well how to spread his *blat* ("largesse") to round up the needed materials. It is he who is celebrated in humorous tales and verse, not the seller, who could be any fool. In that world there is an excess demand for goods, and the buyer must play the role of an aggressive suitor trying to overcome the sales resistance of a coy seller. Just as the Eskimo has a multitude of words to describe the different varieties of snow, so the Russian salesclerk, as she rolls up her eyes and looks off into the distance, has many ways of saying no; *nyet, sevodnya nyet, ne bivaet, nekogda ne bivaet* ("there are not," "right now there are not," "there usually are not," "there never are") are common expressions heard daily in every Soviet department store. In the land of the five-year plan — and the much longer than five-year wait for a car — the buyer can consider himself fortunate if the "car salesman" (such an expression barely exists in Russian, and the words sound exotically foreign) condescends even to see him without special favors. So it is not difficult to understand the leisurely pace of technological progress in the Soviet automobile industry, the rather restrained concern about quality, and the reason why service is nonexistent.[5]

There is also an important historical and political side to the fact that the prevailing mode of the capitalist system is an excess supply of goods. Rosa Luxemburg, J. A. Hobson, Lenin, Leonard Woolf, and others have stated that economic imperialism and much of international economic conflict (especially in the late nineteenth and early twentieth centuries) are due to the persistent expansionary search for new export markets abroad to replace "limited" or "saturated" domestic markets.[6] Such ideas, I believe, have their ultimate origins more in the concepts being stressed here than in some kind of stagnationist underconsumption. Mercantilist forms of trade policy also undoubtedly owe much to the idea that domestic sellers are always putting pressure on the government to protect and expand their markets.

To sum up, the capitalist system has an excellent record on the side of eagerly supplying an abundance of varied goods to those who can afford to buy them. And consumers are free to choose, if only they have the requisite purchasing power. So two cheers for capitalism! Where the record of the market economies is not so good, and sometimes becomes downright disgraceful, is on the employment and income-distribution side — on the side of putting people to work producing goods and earning income so that they can afford to enjoy what comes from spending money.

If only there were a way to encourage firms to recruit more workers as eagerly as they chase after more buyers — if there were a way to institutionalize an excess demand for labor alongside the excess supply of goods — then the market economies could have the best of both worlds. Workers, as well as consumers, would be free to choose. Then capitalism might truly have the last hurrah.

4
The Wage System in a Changing World

PERHAPS THE MOST SIGNIFI-cant difference between the labor market and most other markets can be described as follows. Firms hire labor by a sort of compact — an explicit or implicit contract whose parameters tend to change fairly slowly or are "sticky" over time. In the long run, in a slow-moving or stationary environment, it perhaps doesn't much matter exactly what kind of compact the partners have agreed to, and stickiness of parameters is not an issue. But these features can matter a great deal in an uncertain, rapidly changing world.

The prevailing wage compact in the United States economy looks something like this. First a wage is set, either jointly by collective bargaining or by the employer alone. (Even if competitive forces ultimately determine the wage level — and this is at most an abstraction of a general tendency — every firm must have *some* wage policy.) Then, in a mode that is either explicitly institutionalized in a contract or else tacitly acknowledged, the employer determines how much labor is hired. There are variations on this theme, but the dominant behavioral pattern is a sticky wage with variable employment.

As we have seen, once the wage is fixed, the firm's profit-maximizing response to changes in demand is largely on the side of quantity rather than price. It is always true that the firm wants to supply more output than is being demanded at any given time, but that by itself is in no way inconsistent with laying off workers when demand is weak. The perpetual desire to sell more to every new customer that can be found is not matched by any corresponding zeal to hire the next unemployed worker who comes along.

How does the wage system perform as an allocator of labor? It can be a perfectly adequate system, as good as any and better than most, if the aggregate economy is basically healthy. It can be a terrible system, broadcasting all the wrong incentive signals, if the economy is in a slump suffering from unemployment, excess capacity, and other symptoms of bad health. So when the wage system is good it is very good, but when it is bad it is awful. Its performance generally depends upon the nature of the uncertainty affecting the economy.

Any firm faces a combination of two kinds of uncertainty. One is firm-specific (or possibly industry-specific), having to do with a particular company or business and largely unrelated to other sectors of the economy. The other kind of uncertainty concerns the general state of aggregate demand and affects almost every firm.

Consider, for example, the automobile industry. A firm

The Wage System in a Changing World

like Chrysler faces many specific uncertainties — the public response to its new models, whether or not it can improve productivity, how soon a particular plant can be retooled, how GM is going to respond to an incursion into its market share, how aggressively Japanese imports are going to be pushed. And then there is also the general state of the economy, which affects demand for all firms' products, including Chrysler's.

Firm-specific uncertainty is like an isolated, localized source of possible infection, whereas general uncertainty concerns the health of the entire organism. The wage system represents a good mechanism for dealing with localized infections — provided the overall economy is basically healthy.

When uncertainty is firm-specific, the independent economic shocks occurring throughout the economy cancel each other out. If one firm is experiencing brisker-than-usual business, another is facing weaker-than-usual demand. If more people are eating Big Macs, fewer are buying hamburger meat from the local supermarket. When savers are putting more cash into money market funds, they are depositing less at banks. Tylenol sales are at the expense of aspirin sales. If short skirts are in fashion, long skirts are out. These kinds of offsetting displacements, from changes in the composition of demand, are happening continually in a normally functioning economy, but are handled so smoothly by the wage system that most of the time we aren't even aware of what is taking place right under our noses.

Given a basically healthy economy, the wage system is an effective mechanism for automatically transferring labor from a place where its marginal value is low to where it has a high marginal value. United States statistics reveal that in any given month there is always a substantial flow of people moving into and out of unemployment, most of whom are in transit between jobs and remain unemployed for a relatively short time. This considerable migration of labor is truly guided as if by an invisible hand when firms merely lay off or offer to hire labor in response to changes in the market demand for their product. By so acting within a wage system, the firm is implicitly weighing the value of what an extra worker can produce for it against the prevailing value of what an extra worker can produce elsewhere. But this is just the sort of calculation that ought to be made to ensure that labor is being efficiently allocated throughout the economy.

The wage system therefore acts like a giant screen fed by an economy-wide conveyor belt, continually sorting out firms by the marginal value of an extra unit of labor, and then redistributing labor from low- to high-value firms. Best of all, this self-regulating is done naturally, automatically, without any bureaucracy or red tape. So the wage system is just what the doctor ordered for dealing with localized infections. But what happens when the patient is really sick?

Then the wage system is bad medicine. When aggregate demand has contracted, for whatever reason, sticky wages mean that almost every firm is laying off workers. The basic rationale for a wage system as a means of encouraging an efficient automatic transfer of labor is thwarted when the entire economy is depressed. The wage system, so elementary and ingenious in good times, becomes a malediction when times are bad. Then it causes people to be without jobs, output to decline, and the standard of living to deteriorate. So that while it is excellent for dealing with alterations in the composition of demand, the wage system is terrible at coping with changes in the overall level of aggregate demand.

The unemployment problem runs deeper than the stickiness issue, however, and implicates the wage system as a whole. It may not suffice simply to "unstick" wages. Even allowing for a somewhat greater degree of money-wage flexibility is probably insufficient per se to help much as a practical measure in motivating a depressed wage economy to rehire its unemployed workers.

Why the particular wage compact I have described should be the foremost contemporary example (although by no means prevalent in all places at all times), from a universe of conceivable compacts, is something of a mystery. This issue has been remarked upon, puzzled over, and, finally, analyzed to death by a sect of academic theorists intent on finding buried in it some shrouded logic not apparent to the rest of the world. At this point it seems fair to say only that there are no convincing mathematical reasons, and there certainly is no consensus. My own opinion is that the problem has been overanalyzed and there is no secret meaning to the observation that usually wages are sticky and firms choose quantities.

Concealed in the attempts of many economic theorists to explain sticky wages and unemployment is an innocuous-looking assumption that agents base their actions on a "rational expectation" (or "unbiased forecast") of the consequences. A rational expectation is the weighted sum of the costs or benefits of every possible outcome, the weights being the probabilities of occurence considering all available information. This sort of approach has many useful applications in decision theoretic situations with well-defined probabilities, but it has almost nothing to do with real-world business cycles.[1] There is nothing rational, in any meaningful sense, about a system throughout history creating waves of mass unemployment and irreversibly losing trillions of dollars of forgone output. What is needed to understand the persistence of the wage system is not one more pseudo-explanation clothed in some form of rational expectations, but just a little commonsense insight into the nature of human frailty.

There is a fundamental distinction between actuarial situations representing well-defined risk processes with a stable structure — in which case it may be reasonable to suppose that rational expectations can be inferred from repeated learning experiences — and the kind of nonrecurrent uncertainty that arises from the absence of reliable information about a nonstationary, continually evolving time series. Most macroeconomic uncertainty legitimately belongs to the second category.[2] Macroeconomic events like future recessions are so subject to irregularly shifting forces, erratic changes, and unforeseen developments that it is not even clear *how* to assign a meaningful probability to them. Lacking a scientific basis on which to form calculable probabilities or to make valid statistical inferences, human beings almost invariably fall back on collectively extrapolating the world they currently know unless there are definite reasons for anticipating a change. We substitute a kind of wishful thinking that the present prosperity will continue, perhaps sensing this is not quite right, yet not knowing what else to do but follow the conventional judgment of the crowd.

The basic rationale for a wage system is rooted deeply in the equilibrium mentality of an economy at full employment. During such times the wage system seems ideal for allocating labor among varying job needs, and nobody cares to think very carefully about contingencies to cover some hypothetical recession in the remote future. If things change and a recession hits, the whole country will be jittery about layoffs and wage cuts. Then no union or employer will be in the mood to change the rules of a game that, as we shall see, is hard to win unless everyone else changes too. So there is never a right time to talk about basic wage reform. It is like the story of the farmer who never fixes the roof of his cottage — because he doesn't need to in good weather and because he can't while it's raining.

A doctrine of extreme fundamentalist economic philosophy argues that every existing economic institution or custom in a market economy has a deep-seated rationale that must be fully understood before any corrective action can be taken. (Incidentally, *after* it is fully understood, according to the doctrine, typically no action will need be taken.) Such followers of the "no free lunch" school will undoubtedly find the message of this book irrelevant — after all, if we have a wage system, they will argue, it must already be an optimal system in some sense or why else would we have it in the first place? There is an economists' joke about economists who look at the world this way: "How many true believers in 'efficient markets' does it take to screw in a lightbulb?" "None — because the market has already done it for them."

Extremists of that faith act like the precocious but obsessive young surgeon who refuses to perform an appendectomy because he doesn't understand why the appendix exists in the first place. The truth is that vestigial organs are present in economic systems as well as in biological ones — despite denials of the possibility based, in both cases, on vague or superficial generalities about Darwinian survival value. Whether or not the immature surgeon understands the ultimate reason for the human appendix is irrelevant, of course, compared to the far more compelling insight that a patient with acute appendicitis can be saved by a routine operation.

The current wage system of compensating labor is a perilous anachronism that needs to be replaced. For when a contractionary impulse hits, not only is the initial response of a wage economy to throw people out of work, but a wage system can deepen a recession, multiplying its adverse consequences until the economy is trapped in a vicious circle of persistent involuntary underutilization of the major factors of production. This public cost of the wage system — its "macroeconomic externality" of misbegotten unemployment spawning further unemployment — is a pollutionlike consequence that private agents have little incentive to consider.

When U.S. Steel shuts down a mill in Pittsburgh, the aftermath radiates throughout the rest of the economy. The unemployed steelworker cannot now afford to buy a GM Chevrolet assembled in Detroit, a GE radio manufactured in Schenectady, a Texas Instruments watch made in Dallas, or that extra case of Budweiser from St. Louis. A ripple of multiplier effects spreads across the entire country, and eventually the world, leaving in its wake further layoffs and plant closings. If a contraction is not stopped early enough, the unemployment can become self-sustaining, and the stagnation becomes a deadly trap. The unemployed steelworker cannot afford to buy a new Chevrolet because GM isn't placing enough orders with U.S. Steel; and GM isn't placing enough orders with U.S. Steel because an unemployed steelworker cannot afford to buy a new Chevrolet.

The primary source of current purchasing power is the current income paid to factors of production, which simultaneously feeds back to constitute demand spending. In the very long run, then, there is a valid sense in which supply creates its own demand and the economy is held at full employment by its own bootstraps. But the existence of money and credit breaks the literal equivalence on any particular market day between aggregate factor-receipts and total sales-proceeds. In a monetary economy the feedback linkage between income and spending can become temporarily uncoupled for a wide variety of reasons. Indeed, a basic theme of modern macroeconomics stresses the great potential volatility of aggregate demand, which in the short run can take on a life of its own.

The typical first cause of an economic contraction is a decrease in investment or some other volatile component of aggregate spending. Whatever the cause, if a recession continues long enough, enormous problems can develop with a wage system. By the time the coupling mechanism is restored, the economy may find itself struggling in that vicious circle, where low employment is causing insufficient spending, which is reinforcing the low employment. The market system may then suffer from a prolonged failure to coordinate the desired consumption and production plans of all its agents throughout the economy, because the unemployed lack the purchasing power to communicate or make effective their potential demands—the demands they would have if they were employed.

In a modern economy, many different goods are produced and consumed. The contemporary firm is a specialist in production, while its workers are generalists in consumption. Workers receive a wage from the firm they work for, but they spend it almost entirely on the products of other firms. To obtain a wage, the unemployed worker must first succeed in being hired. But no firm is about to hire the unemployed worker during a recession. When demand is depressed, because there is so much unemployment, curtailed purchasing power, and little spending, no firm sees how it can profitably market the increased output of an extra worker.

Like a self-fulfilling prophecy, once the expectation of aggregate demand associated with a given unemployment level becomes ingrained, it turns into a major cause of its own persistence. If plants are closed and business confidence is damaged, the condition tends to replicate itself. This sort of stagnation effect lies behind every drawn-out recession and was almost surely the main source of the inertia that kept the Great Depression in place, although economists to this day argue about its causes.

5
Keynes and the Wage Issue

THE GREAT DEPRESSION OF the 1930s was the worst crisis the capitalist system had ever undergone. It was a troubling time, as anyone who lived through it will testify. There had been other depressions, some very serious, but none of that depth or duration.

In the United States, one fourth of the labor force was unemployed—well before any meaningful safety net existed. Total output fell by a third. Germany fared even worse, with terrifying consequences. It is no exaggeration to say that Hitler could not have attained power except for the depression. Great Britain suffered relatively less during the 1930s, but on the other hand had also been stagnating during the 1920s. The list goes on and on. Everywhere throughout the industrial capitalist world, factories were closed and workers were jobless. The economic cost of the Great Depression was staggering — a loss of goods and services of roughly the same order of magnitude as the cost of all the economic resources used up during World War II.

But even beyond the horrible material casualties, there was something especially gruesome about the Great Depression. The casualties were not suffered for any cause — they were manifestly purposeless, meaningless, unnecessary. Over there is a closed-down shoe factory, boarded up for lack of buyers. Over here are unemployed workers who want jobs and need shoes but can't afford to pay for them. So what or who in this crazy system is keeping them apart? Could anything possibly be more embarrassing for capitalism? The economic experts, those peerless artistes of the status quo who never lost an opportunity to tout the "miracle of the market," didn't appear to have any remedies. The only thing they seemed to agree about was the overriding need for the government to balance its budget.

One lesson we have learned clearly from history is that people will not stand idly by in the face of acute economic frustration; they want decisive action, and if one government won't give it to them they'll find a government that will. An astute politician, Franklin D. Roosevelt, echoed the mood of his times when he spoke out in his first inaugural address: "This nation asks for action, and action now . . . We must act and act quickly." The only problem was that neither Roosevelt nor anyone else had an overall plan of action; no one really understood what was wrong or how to cure it.

Where were the economists during the crisis? They were, by and large, sitting on the sidelines. The were even more perplexed than most, since as a rule they were committed to an economic doctrine that held such things as mass unemployment to be impossible. So the economists were viewed as irrelevant fiddlers scratching out old tunes about how laissez faire ought to work while the economy itself was burning to the ground.

In the middle of this macabre setting, in late 1935, the English economist John Maynard Keynes finished writing a seemingly arcane professional manuscript on economic theory. It was destined to become one of the most important books published in this century.[1] The basic message of *The General Theory of Employment, Interest and Money* was that a modern capitalist economy is not the automatically self-regulating system almost everyone had thought (or at least claimed) it to be. The fundamental natural forces tending toward equilibrium, if they exist, operate much too slowly on an aggregate level and need to be supplemented by quicker and less painful remedies. Discretionary government spending (such as public works), taxation, and monetary policy should be used in the context of a "mixed economy" deliberately to *create* full employment.

Although Keynes's revolutionary book introduced many new ideas, it is no accident that *The General Theory* starts out with the wage issue. To classical economists, persistent unemployment of labor meant basically one thing — that the wage rate is too high.

Has anyone ever seen in the supermarket a potato that is "unemployed"? As buyers we never observe a persistent oversupply of potatoes. At one time or another a particular supermarket may be overstocked, just as others are understocked, but that is a temporary derangement. If the overall supply of potatoes increased, or the demand decreased, the price would automatically decline to clear the potato market. The only way an oversupply of potatoes could ever be observed would be if somehow the price of potatoes were artificially set "too high." The nearest we ever come to this is an agricultural price-support program, in which case the oversupply shows itself as a stockpile of inventories held by (or for) the government.

The classical economists generally regarded the labor market as fundamentally no different from any other market. Recessions were mere temporary disturbances of credit and confidence. So long as wages were flexible, there should be no more persistent tendency for labor to be unemployed than for potatoes to be unemployed. As A. C. Pigou, a distinguished economist of world stature, Keynes's teacher, and the foremost representative of the prevailing orthodoxy, put it in 1933 at the very bottom of the worst depression in history: "Such unemployment as exists at any time is due wholly to the fact that changes in demand conditions are continually taking place and that frictional resistances prevent the appropriate wage adjustments from being made instantaneously."[2] If workers were unemployed, it meant that labor costs were too high and there was nothing the government could, or should, do aside from possibly urging that wages be cut more vigorously.

Keynes disagreed fundamentally, almost violently, with the classical approach. "The matters at issue are of an importance which cannot be exaggerated" he wrote in the preface, describing his book as "an attempt by an economist to bring to an issue the deep divergences of opinion between fellow economists which have for the time being almost destroyed the practical influence of economic theory and will, until they are resolved, continue to do so." What Keynes objected to was not so much the abstract description of "too high" wages as a cause of unemployment (although he didn't at all like that way of putting the matter), as it was the complacent implication that there is nothing better to do than sit around waiting for wages to come down. In an important chapter entitled "Changes in Money Wages," whose content has not been significantly improved upon to this day, Keynes mounted a devastating attack on the classical position.

In the previous example, an oversupply of potatoes can be easily corrected by lowering their price. But this is because the market for potatoes is rather isolated, with limited feedback effects on the rest of the economy. The big difference between potatoes and labor, which all the classicists seemed to have missed, is that 80 percent of national income is not spent on potatoes, but on labor. Keynes picked up this theme and hammered it home.

An isolated reduction in money-wage rates for any one particular firm or industry will induce that particular firm or industry to employ more workers, because costs are reduced while demand is unaffected. But this partial-equilibrium story (which apparently is what the classical economists had in mind) cannot be generalized to the level of an entire economy without committing a serious "fallacy of composition." The problem is that an all-round cut in money wages feeds right back to the spending side, where it constitutes a significant lowering of general purchasing power. Whether or not aggregate demand will fall proportionately more or less than the original wage cut depends upon a long list of possible causes and effects, many of which Keynes analyzed in some detail, coming in the end to an agnostic position. Contemporary economists might disagree with some of Keynes's emphases, would add some additional effects to his list, and probably have fewer doubts that wage reductions will *eventually* decrease unemployment.[3] But there is still very little question that wage changes constitute a painful, roundabout, inefficient, slow, and hardly automatic way of maintaining full employment.

Besides, reducing wages and prices relative to a fixed money supply, Keynes pointed out, is tantamount to increasing the money supply relative to fixed wages and prices. As a purely practical matter, discretionary fiscal and monetary policy represents a far more pragmatic way to attack unemployment than any conceivable series of wage reductions. If the public is not able to spend enough to support full-employment production, let the government do it for them.

The effect of the Keynesian critique was profound. Pigou himself conceded as much when he wrote, a year after *The General Theory*: "Until recently no economist doubted that an all-round reduction in the rate of money wages might be expected to increase, and an all-round enhancement to diminish, the volume of employment."[4] Like a great magician, Keynes removed the wage issue from center stage and replaced it by discretionary government policy to manage aggregate demand.

In the long course of history I think this disappearing act must increasingly come to be viewed as something of a dazzling digression from the main route to economic prosperity. Detours are necessary, of course, when the primary road is impassable (and, let us hope, being repaired). But no matter how rough and intractable it may appear at first glance, sooner or later the wage issue must be confronted head on. How labor is paid remains the central issue. And in our time stagflation has returned it to center stage with a vengeance.

The Keynesian victory represented as complete a conquest by "an idea whose time has come" as was ever witnessed; and it happened so suddenly that it was truly a revolution. Gone within a decade was the complacency of do-nothing laissez-faire economics, with its fatalistic attitude toward deep depression and mass unemployment. In its place the Keynesian revolution preached the positive gospel of the mixed economy where, in the words of the U.S. Employment Act of 1946, "it is the continuing responsibility of the federal government to . . . promote maximum employment, production and purchasing power" and to maintain "conditions under which there will be offered useful employment opportunities . . . for those able, willing and seeking to work." The "balanced budget" was replaced by "compensatory" or "functional" finance — the avowed use of government expenditures and taxes to raise aggregate demand whenever required to promote full employment and growth, purposely increasing the deficit if necessary. Activist monetary policy (primarily open market operations by the central bank to determine the stock of money and, ultimately, interest rates) evolved into a widely accepted policy tool for achieving macroeconomic goals. The relevant debate became not whether the government should participate in economic affairs, but rather how government can participate most effectively.

If the new ideas needed any confirmation, history soon provided a dramatic test. With the greatly increased government spending just before and during World War II came a tremendous surge of output and employment. (Indeed, Nazi Germany's rearmament program had shown the same effects much earlier.) The unemployment rate in the United States went from a high of 25 percent to a low of less than 1 percent. So convincing was this experiment that most people feared the economy would slide back into depression once the wartime spending ended. But it didn't happen that way.

Taken as a whole, the postwar growth record of the advanced capitalist countries has been extremely impressive, certainly much better than anybody had a right to expect. No one doubts that the capitalist countries have turned a critical corner since the Keynesian revolution. Really deep depressions are a thing of the past, preventable by timely fiscal and monetary policy. The economic problems we now face are very serious, but it is important to see them in proper historical perspective. Neither stagflation nor any other current malady is comparable to such a grave economic catastrophe as the Great Depression. The grinding poverty and pervasive destitution of the bleak 1930s is no longer a haunting image of reality. That we now have the knowledge, the tools, the institutions, and the will to prevent prolonged depressions represents an achievement of the highest order.

This having been said, it must also be recorded that the high tide of enthusiastic Keynesian activism has crested. At one time the "new economics" seemed to hold out the hope of being able to fine-tune an economy on a more or less continuous track of reasonably full employment. But an unreliable model structure, long and variable lags, unstable behavioral relations, shifting expectations, and politics have conspired to turn stabilization policy (and also forecasting) into a treacherous game that has ended up badly off the mark many times. Hitting a macroeconomic target with the aggregate policy instruments currently available has not exactly turned out to be like shooting fish in a barrel. Sometimes it seems more like trying to harpoon by moonlight an Atlantic eel wriggling through stormy seas.

In the end, Keynesian macrotheory has not worked out to be nearly so refined as once expected. Rather, it more closely resembles a kind of rough and ready defense that can be reliably put in place to stop major disturbances from turning into deep prolonged depressions. In this backstopping role alone Keynesian policy represents an extraordinarily significant accomplishment, even if it turns out to be too crude for fine tuning.

There is an important postscript to the Keynesian episode. Keynes made very little mention of inflation in his book. That seemed natural enough under the circumstances. *The General Theory*, after all, dealt essentially with the case of underemployed resources. Keynes, along with almost everybody else, didn't imagine there could be significant inflation until the economy approached full employment. (In fact, nominal wages and prices fell significantly during the Great Depression.)

Gradually during the postwar period, but with relentlessly accelerating vigor over the last two decades, that pattern has changed. For reasons we don't yet entirely comprehend, upward pressure on prices and wages now appears well before labor markets become tight or capacity is fully utilized. James Meade has put the matter as follows: "Keynes, if anyone, can be regarded as the architect of the system designed to maintain effective real demand at the full-employment level. Would that he were alive to exercise his ingenious and fertile mind on the problem to which the very success of his construction has in large measure contributed, — namely the problem of making a high and sustained level of *real* economic activity compatible with a restraint of those inflationary rises in *money* prices and wage rates which are so naturally demanded and so readily conceded in conditions of a sustained high level of demand for the goods and services in question."[5]

This new pattern of creeping inflation, poorly understood, not honestly predicted by any theory, and just not supposed to happen, has wreaked havoc on the standard Keynesian prescriptions. It has thrown the public and the economics profession (despite the brave front put up by some economists) into a state of disarray, even bewilderment, not seen since the early days of the Great Depression some fifty years ago.[6] Now, as then, embarrassing questions about what to do are being asked but not convincingly answered. There is an increasing perception that unadulterated macroeconomic policy may constitute a losing hand, and the time has come to deal a new one.

6

An Uninvited Guest Who Came to Stay

THE WILD CARD IN THE CURrent deck, the joker that upsets all the economic calculations, is inflation.

Suppose we were examining a century-and-a-half-long time series of economic indicators from the United States or any other advanced capitalist economy. We would be struck by the following pattern. While the post–World War II epoch is marked by comparatively high employment, growth, and stability in the real economy, it is also noteworthy for a strong upward drift in prices unprecedented during an era of peace. In the past, most peacetime periods featured prolonged spells of deflation—in the real economy and also in the price level. On average, over good years and bad, the price level was more stable but the real economy less so.

Keynesian theory implied there ought to be an "inflationary discontinuity" at full employment. With unemployed factors of production strewn all over the landscape, there should be no good reason for costs and prices to rise. But once full employment is reached, any injection of additional purchasing power has nowhere to go but into price increases — resulting in demand-pull inflation. Of course, no one believed the boundary line was that finely drawn. For one thing, no economist knows exactly what percentage of the labor force constitutes "full employment." (There are always some transitional workers looking for jobs.) The demarcation between economic expansion and inflation was viewed as more of a gray area than a fine line. Still, the basic thesis of demand-pull inflation was generally accepted: inflation is primarily a situation of too much money chasing too few goods.

It was recognized early on, therefore, that fine tuning was going to be difficult if the aim was simply to hit full employment without causing inflation. As it turned out, that was a wildly optimistic way of looking at the problem. Very few economists were able to foresee just how tough a dilemma was lurking in the form of a nasty "cost-push" inflation that would pose some unpleasant choices between employment and price stability.

The proximate cause of the new inflation is a cost-push, wage-price spiral that feeds on its own momentum and expectations. If wages rise, prices must go up. But if prices are expected to increase, wages will be set that much higher to compensate. Each union and company must do what everybody else is doing just to protect its relative standing. No group wins a bigger piece of the pie of real goods and services from this frustrating game of anticipation and reaction. There is no evidence, for example, that militant collective bargaining actually raises labor's real share; on the contrary, it seems that raising money wages merely leads to inflationary increases in the prices of goods workers buy. Cost-push inflation is essentially a vicious circle for everyone, workers and capitalists alike.

This is similar to the reaction of a crowd in a baseball stadium when the home team is behind by a run, there are two outs in the bottom of the ninth, with a runner on second and the local hero stepping up to the plate. First a few fans stand up to get a better view of the big play. This blocks the view of the people seated directly behind, so they stand up too. Soon all the fans are on their feet. Each spectator is worse off when they are all standing than when they are all sitting. But this knowledge does not prevent the crowd from rising en masse and remaining on its feet. In the case of inflation, however, it is difficult to get the audience to sit down again; either an austere fiscal and monetary policy must make the environment too uncomfortable for anyone to want to stand, or an incomes policy must individually force each person to sit down and stay put.

Gradually since about 1965, we have become increasingly aware that the advanced capitalist economies are suffering from a new disorder — stagflation, the simultaneous existence of inflation and unemployment. Furthermore, although it is still too early for decisive pronouncements, it appears that the disease has been getting worse over time. Business cycles in the postwar period have shown rising inflation and unemployment from one cycle to the next. The sum of inflation plus unemployment, the so-called misery index, has approximately doubled from about 7 percent in the early 1960s to around 14 percent over the last several years.

But why is inflation included in the misery index? Unemployment belongs because, when people are out of work, the economy is deprived of the real goods and services they could be producing. Does inflation make people feel miserable in an analogous way?

The answer is basically no. There are few direct costs of inflation. In a perfectly anticipated, balanced inflation, where all prices and wages (and debts) go up by the same proportion, in principle everyone has the same real purchasing power and can consume exactly the same menu of goods and services independent of the inflation rate. Of course inflation is not balanced or perfectly anticipated, but it seems hard to believe that genuine misery is arising *solely* from imbalance or imperfect anticipation. Rather, people seem genuinely to dislike the inflation itself. Economists condescendingly refer to this attitude as "money illusion," but the public seems to think that inflation represents a loss of purchasing power every bit as real as the loss of goods and services accompanying unemployment.

Unanticipated inflation, coming after loan contracts have been written in nominal terms, does redistribute wealth, from creditors to debtors. But the net effect on the community is zero. (Leave aside misers hoarding large amounts of cash under their mattresses.) Many solid middle-class citizens (say owners of fixed-mortgage homes) actually benefit from unanticipated inflation. In fact it is surprisingly hard to make valid generalizations about which actual groups (poor, rich, blacks, whites, employed, unemployed, workers, capitalists, old, young) are harmed or helped by inflation.

An Uninvited Guest Who Came To Stay

There seems to be a strong "us versus them" illusion out there when it comes to inflation. The good things that happen to us — higher wages, less effort to meet our mortgage payments, and such — are due to our own virtue or our own luck. If only they (meaning the government) could learn to keep down the prices of things we buy, could get their hands out of our pockets, maybe we could actually enjoy our good fortune instead of having it taken away at every turn.

Of course there are other aspects. There is the legitimate apprehension that, if a line isn't drawn somewhere, creeping inflation will accelerate and get out of hand — so that not to deal with the current inflation now is just to put off dealing with an even worse inflation later. There are those genuine redistributions of wealth and income under actual inflation which no economist may be able to identify as materially affecting any particular group of people, but which are certainly affecting specific individuals. There is a somewhat vague sense that the social order is disrupted by inflation, that society is somehow being undermined when the currency is debased. There are actual distortions caused by a tax system whose rates are fixed in nominal terms. And then there are the tangible real costs of inflation: changing price lists, updated menus and catalogs, more frequent trips to the bank, although these are small losses by any reckoning.

The bottom line is that the public feels an aversion to inflation whether or not it is valid and whether or not economic theory adequately explains it. That aversion has very important policy implications. If wages and prices are pushed up even during times of stagnation, a cruel policy dilemma is created.

Given our present institutional structure, the only reliable prescription for getting rid of inflation is a dose of old-time religion: some combination of tight money, high interest rates, low government spending, or high taxes calculated to bring on a good stiff contraction that will discipline wage demands and break inflationary expectations. This is the notorious "policy-induced recession" — and the good news is that it works. The bad news is that this kind of medicine creates unemployment, negative growth, and business failures. The mass layoffs, plant closings, and bankruptcies fall especially unevenly on those groups (and regions) conscripted to serve as inflation fighters for the rest of the economy. (A disproportionate impact on certain sectors of the economy — especially construction, consumer durables, and capital goods — is a general problem of almost any aggregate macroeconomic policy.)

Once a government starts down the old-time-religion path, it has frequently been forced to back off in midcourse, or at a point before the inflation is wrung out, because the protest over the ensuing stagnation becomes too much to bear politically. Even if inflation is halted, the hiatus is only temporary. At *some* point a different government, or maybe a differently oriented version of the same one, will try to rectify the damage to the real economy by changing course to an expansionary policy. But heating up the economy typically brings back the inflation, sooner or later, along with the jobs and the goods and services. After a few rounds of this sort of political business cycle the economy is occasionally somewhat better, but frequently worse, than when it started. In the meantime, the stop-go battle against one arm or the other of stagflation has spilled over to disrupt the foreign-trade balance, the government budget, capital investment, and productivity.

What is the root cause of stagflation? No one really

knows why the mixed economies appear to be harboring larger amounts of inflation along with unemployment. Every aspect of inflation seems poorly understood at this point, if we are honest about it.

For some economists, growth of the money stock is the key to understanding, as echoed by Milton Friedman's war cry, "Inflation is always and everywhere a monetary phenomenon."[1] This much is indisputable about the extreme monetarist position: cost-push inflation could not long endure without the acquiescense of an expanded money supply any more than an inelastic balloon can be blown up. But is the elastic money supply *causing* the inflation, or is it more an *accommodation* by the central bankers (without which unemployment would result) to underlying wage-price pressure? Whereas cost-push inflation has been condoned, and to that extent facilitated, by an easy-money policy, that is very different from postulating, as the extreme monetarists do, the existence of a direct mechanical causality going from the quantity of money to the price level. My own opinion, shared by the majority of economists, is that while some kind of joint causality ultimately underlies all such phenomena, in this case the main strand runs from changes in incomes and prices caused by other factors to accommodations in the quantity of money. (The "quantity of money," incidentally, is not a terribly operational concept in the first place, as Federal Reserve Chairman Paul Volcker and others who have attempted to control particular monetary aggregates have learned the hard way.)

Many eclectic economists see behind the inflation of the last two decades an isolated series of bad breaks: the Vietnam war, exogeneous oil-price increases, harvest failures, and so forth. Still other original-sin reasons for inflation are frequently offered: too much government spending, too much regulation, too much union power, too much big business, too much indexing of incomes to consumer prices, too much self-fulfilling expectation of inflation itself. Sometimes it seems that there are almost as many explanations as there are economists. Probably there is no totally convincing single reason or sole cause, but rather a variety of reasons and causes.

Yet, while our ability to explain or predict inflation in any given year is notoriously poor, it does seem to me (and others) that there is an ominous kind of internal logic to the overall process of stagflation. Step back for a moment and look at the issue in international and historical perspective. After more than a century of relatively inflation-free development, inflation has become a stubborn problem everywhere in the capitalist world. Why? Posing the issue globally this way prompts another question. Has not capitalism itself changed in some fundamental structural way that causes, or at least encourages, a new inflationary tendency?

Although little more than an unproved intuition at this point, one diagnosis of stagflation seems somewhat more significant, as well as more chilling, than the others. Everywhere throughout the capitalist world economic growth has become an acknowledged high priority responsibility of government. The fundamental reason for the inflationary disposition of the global economic order is that, in the post-Keynesian period, capitalism has become a relatively more compassionate or softer-hearted system. Not only have they opted to cast a fairly broad safety net for the unemployed in their midst, but the citizens of democratic mixed economies everywhere will not long tolerate high unemployment rates. The reelection of Prime Minister Margaret Thatcher in 1983 is the kind of exception that proves the rule.

Paul A. Samuelson has stated the case rather starkly: "I believe that the present inflation is rooted deep in the nature of the mixed economy . . . we live in the Age After Keynes. Electorates all over the world have eaten of the fruit of the tree of modern economic knowledge and there is no going back to an earlier age. High employment or full employment is everywhere a goal insisted upon by the electorate of all political persuasions. A half century ago there was no comparable political sentiment effective against incurring prolonged depression or even stagnation; rather there was often a preoccupation with the perils of inflation, of budget and foreign trade deficits. This shift in populist attitudes of governments necessarily shifts the odds against stable prices (and of course against falling prices). No longer can one expect half the peacetime years to experience falling prices. If general price levels rarely stand still and often rise, then the secular trend of prices must be upward on the average."[2]

Robert M. Solow has put the same idea this way: "Workers and employers nowadays fear prolonged recession and mass unemployment less than they used to, *and they are right*. These things are very unlikely to happen. Modern governments know how to prevent major depressions, they have the legislative and administrative tools they need in order to apply their knowledge, and they have the motivation: No government could survive in an advanced democracy if it permitted a major depression and serious unemployment on a scale that occurred more or less regularly in the good old days. So 1932 will not come around again, and there is not much reason to look for those forms of behavior that were conditioned by the ever-present possibility that it might."[3]

When workers and employers think recessions are going to be short and mild because the government is going to bail them out, that belief itself is very likely to impart a serious overall inflationary bias to the economy. If the "good old days" of deep, prolonged depressions meant no general tendencies toward either price inflation or price deflation, what does it do to the inertia of wage-price expectations to build into the system an ever more solid ratchet that doesn't allow the wheel to turn toward deflation, but leaves it free to rotate the other way?

Should this diagnosis be basically correct, it is troubling. For it would mean that there might be something structural about stagflation. The humane full-employment policy bias of a modern mixed economy may contain certain contradictions with price stability and may therefore have some tendency to become self-destructive when it is applied over a long time. In that case the new inflation is not just a freak mishap, but is more like the serious long-term side effect of a sustained dosage of Keynesian full-employment medicine. A capitalist economy can enjoy full employment or price stability, but not both simultaneously—and the tradeoff between them deteriorates when too much of Keynes's cure is applied. Stagflation is likely to remain a grave affliction unless something fundamental changes. So the prognosis from this line of reasoning appears grim, barring the development of some new antistagflation medication or vaccine.

Whatever the root causes of the new inflation, and it is appropriate to reemphasize that we simply do not know what they definitely are, the public clamors for a solution.

An Uninvited Guest Who Came To Stay

What, then, is the best way to combat inflation? Again there sometimes seem to be almost as many prescriptions as there are economists. Here are the main ones:

1. *Tight money.* This was covered in talking about old-time religion. It works, but the trouble is that the cure is worse than the disease.

2. *Do nothing.* This doesn't seem to be politically feasible, and the inflation problem won't go away by itself. (Quite the opposite, there is every indication that a policy of benign neglect will accelerate inflation.)

3. *Index everything.* This approach attempts to live with inflation rather than trying to fight it. If wages, pensions, and most other contracts are fully indexed to the cost of living so as to guarantee real purchasing power, the argument goes, the public will not care so much about inflation and the government can concentrate on improving real economic performance. To some extent we have already moved in this direction by having cost-of-living-adjustment clauses in about half of major union contracts and in most social security benefit payments. One drawback is that it is impossible to index everything. Another is that indexing tends to accelerate inflation, not control it, so that if the inflation per se is bothersome this will only exacerbate the problem. (Heavily indexed countries like Israel tend to have tremendous rates of inflation which are very difficult to bring under control.) For every economist who wants more escalator clauses, there seem to be at least two who blame these clauses for a good part of the current inflation and want to ban them altogether.

4. *Synchronize collective bargaining.* In the United States and Canada, wage setting is relatively decentralized and unsynchronized. As a result, nominal wages respond more slowly to unemployment and to price movements than

in Western Europe and Japan. If collective wage bargaining were more centralized, as in the other OECD countries, the parties might be better able to see what they are doing in light of the overall macroeconomic situation. Some observers in the United States, therefore, suggest legislation to make our own wage-setting process more synchronized and more frequent. The problem with this approach is that it is a two-edged sword. More responsive nominal wages are desirable in deflationary periods, but undesirable during inflationary upswings. The historical record does not readily indicate whether, other things being equal, synchronous wage setting actually yields better macroeconomic performance.

5. *Wage-price controls.* Most people hate them. A large bureaucracy is needed to administer the program, create detailed norms, and monitor compliance. Wage-price controls pose endless dilemmas of how this or that specific wage or price of this or that specific company shall be treated when the economy's structure has changed. Moreover, controlled prices result in shortages of goods, a phenomenon toward which the American public has shown itself to be intolerant. The postwar experience of several mixed economies that experimented with wage-price controls has not, on the whole, been very encouraging. There may be a legitimate short-period function for controls as part of a coordinated inflation-fighting strategy, but they are probably not viable in peacetime as a long-term device.

6. *Tax-based incomes policy (TIP).* This would offer tax incentives to firms and workers to keep prices and wages low. TIP is really just a form of wage-price control where the penalty system is more flexible. Essentially the same norm-setting dilemmas and bureaucratic problems are involved—if anything, it is more complicated to administer

TIP than wage-price controls because the exact degree of compliance must now be monitored. (One-sided TIP programs aimed at controlling wages alone are considerably easier to administer, but even they are unwieldy when it gets down to practical details, besides being widely perceived as having an antilabor bias.) Despite the drawbacks, some form of TIP is arguably the best of the current batch of alternatives.

This list could be extended, but the point remains that there are no obvious solutions. It is all too easy to be critical of one or another proposed reform. Yet to be negative about every constructive proposal is to favor the current political business cycle. The honest question is this: If you must choose the least unacceptable among many unsatisfactory alternatives, which one do you select?

I want to offer for consideration a different approach to fighting stagflation — not just a quick fix but a permanent solution. This way preserves the advantages of decentralized decision making with its intrinsic flexibility but promises to be a die-hard natural enemy of unemployment and inflation. When a market system is freed from the mold of standard wage-compensation formulas, and large firms are paying their employees by any one of several different share formulas, the fundamental macroeconomic performance of the system improves quite dramatically.

7
Back to Basics

Although the wage system is the predominant mode of compensation in the United States and in most other advanced capitalist countries, it is hardly a universal system, over time or across space.

Even in the United States today, a large part of the earnings of tens of millions of workers is a direct share of the value of what they produce or what is produced by the organization they work for. Self-employed workers and professionals (farmers, small contractors, doctors and lawyers in private practice), many executives, people who work on commission (salespeople in many activities, including real estate, insurance, securities), people who receive tips (waiters, hairdressers, taxi drivers), and many others are all directly paid a share of the value of output. As compared with industrial work, employment in such professions seems much more immune from recessions. It is no coincidence that almost anyone at any time can get a job selling magazine subscriptions on commission. Although this kind of observation may seem trivial, it contains an important clue as to why certain organizations are willing to expand employment, while others are not.

Japan offers a living laboratory for many of the ideas in this book. Like other natural experiments, the Japanese example is not pure or controlled — so there is room for several interpretations, one of which is quite compatible with the broad outlines of my thesis.

The Japanese economy in the postwar period has turned in what can only be described as a spectacular performance. Living on a remote volcanic island chain half a world removed from the other advanced industrialized countries, totally dependent on imports for every basic raw material and ultimately relying on their ability to penetrate and subjugate the harsh environment of foreign marketplaces, the Japanese have built a towering economic colossus on the ruins of World War II. Their macroeconomic record has featured relatively moderate inflation, extremely low unemployment, and unbelievably high sustained growth rates of output and productivity. Their ability to stabilize employment and income in the face of recession has been remarkable — especially for an economy so vulnerably dependent on foreign trade. Japan weathered the contractionary storms of 1954, 1957-58, 1962, 1965, 1971, 1974-75, 1981-1983, with relatively little change in registered unemployment. No other capitalist economy can boast that kind of record, and the prewar Japanese economy could not either.[1]

Many have noted that Japanese labor markets seem to be fundamentally, almost culturally, different from their Western counterparts. A prominent feature of the system is that large firms appear to offer lifetime employment to their regular employees — the famed *shūshin koyō* system. One comparative sociological study after another documents how well Japanese workers are treated by management, with excellent working conditions (including attempts at making work more interesting and meaningful), a sympathetic attitude toward illness, death, or other misfortunes, and benefits such as marriage and family allowances, educational loans for children, housing subsidies, good one-class, integrated company cafeterias, sports clubs, and vacation resorts.[2] Nathan Glazer states flatly that "the Japanese factory or company is at present the most egalitarian in the world, outside China."[3] Workers and managers are frequently dressed similarly on the job, use the informal pattern of speech, eat in the same place, and are paid in the same form. Workers respond with corporate loyalty and a positive attitude toward productivity-enhancing technological improvements. Although it is possible to exaggerate such features, the Japanese workplace does seem to be fundamentally different from its Western counterpart.

In the postwar period, the *shūshin koyō* worker is paid by, negotiates for, and thinks in terms of a base monthly salary — not an hourly wage. In addition, most regular industrial workers are paid a significant fraction of their pay in the form of a twice yearly profit-sharing bonus. The bonuses can be quite large, sometimes worth up to five months or more of salary in a good year for the company. On the average, over a fourth of a Japanese industrial worker's total remuneration consists of bonus payments.

Bonus income is a significant component of national income. Japanese corporations pay out more in bonuses than they end up making in after-bonus profits.

The essence of the bonus system is the idea that the pay of corporate employees to some extent depends, or at least is widely perceived as depending, on the corporation's market performance. That this *perception* of the bonus is widespread within Japan seems hardly disputable. Skeptical observers question whether bonus payments actually vary with profitability. When this position is taken to an extreme, it seems to miss the point.

The Japanese bonus is not a form of disguised wage. The mere fact that bonuses are segregated from salaries — legally, traditionally, and even linguistically possessing a separate status — suggests that *shūshin koyō* workers think of themselves more as permanently employed partners than as hired hands. The Japanese term for "contractual cash earnings" (salary) is "the wage that is surely paid" *(kimatte shikyūsuru kyūyo)*. The "special cash payment" (bonus), by contrast, is defined in official statistics as a payment made to the worker "temporarily, unexpectedly, or erratically at the discretion of the employer independent of any previous agreement, contract, or rule."

Although the degree of bonus flexibility is perhaps not so great as is sometimes supposed, neither is it negligible. The bonus system provides the Japanese employer with an important means of reducing labor costs during recessions. Bonuses, like dividends, do respond to corporate earnings, but with a complicated lag structure not easy to quantify by any rigidly prescribed rule.

Is the Japanese system culturally or economically determined? It is tempting for me to argue that the prime mover here is the bonus system — that once it is in place (for rea-

sons of historical accident, cultural inclination, or whatever else) economic forces are set in motion that bring about
many of the other remarkable features of the Japanese
industrial landscape. I do not wish to overstate this case.
Surely there are also elements of more complicated causality operating here so that at most there can be talk of "pre-
dispositions" or "reinforcing tendencies." Yet, when all is
said and done, I must regard the opposite extreme — that
there is no truth at all to this basic thesis — as highly im-
plausible. That the only industrial economy in the world
with anything remotely resembling a share system should
also display all the broad tendencies predicted by the
theory strikes me as too much of a coincidence to write off
entirely to cultural determinism.

After all, contrary to popular impressions, most of the
unique "cultural" features of the Japanese labor market
are not ancient and assuredly do not stretch back to feudal
times. They first appear, or at least first become pronounced, comparatively recently — only after World War
II, just when the economy's overall performance dramatically improves. The Japanese economy, including its labor
markets, does not appear to have been nearly so different
from the other advanced industrial economies in the period
before the war. Although possessing a very impressive
growth rate ever since the Meiji restoration, prewar Japan
suffered like any other economy from frequent and severe
cyclical fluctuations, spells of unemployment, and even periods of relative stagnation. There is no evidence that the
prewar Japanese labor market was fundamentally different from other labor markets throughout the capitalist
world. It has been well documented that lifetime employment, the bonus system, and the special treatment of

workers barely existed before the end of the war. Japan may have provided fertile soil, but the plant was not yet growing. Only in the postwar years, perhaps building on certain prewar tendencies and traditions, does the unique Japanese labor market system begin to emerge as a significantly distinct pattern.[4]

In earlier times throughout the world, share systems were the predominant mode of labor payment rather than the exception. In preindustrial agriculture, sharecropping was the prevalent method of remunerating hired labor. There have always been professions that pay money wages (building craftsmen, for example), but this is probably because it is difficult to measure directly the value of output. Such jobs represent an insignificant exception in a preindustrial world where most workers, even the small fraction not engaged in agriculture, are either self-employed or paid in kind.

In many areas of the world today a share system remains the primary payment mechanism for the gathering of natural harvests and for agricultural activities. Wherever sharecropping is practiced, the landowner never voluntarily turns away a willing worker. Whatever bad things can be said about sharecropping, involuntary unemployment of labor is not one of them. From the owner's point of view, there are always unfilled labor vacancies available and the more croppers the better. The share proportion paid by the landowner generally depends upon the fertility of the land and the alternative earning power of the tenant.[5]

The industrial revolution brought forth a new phenomenon — the large-scale, high-productivity industrial enterprise based on division of labor. With the factory system came a need to apply new rules for dividing the income pie.

The wage system was by no means the only mode of labor payment used throughout the mines and mills of the nascent revolution.

The first country to industrialize was Great Britain. The heart and soul of heavy industry are coal and steel. British coal- and steelworkers were not paid straight money wages at first. Rather they were paid according to a system called the "sliding scale," by a formula that linked their pay directly to the value of what their firm produced. If output prices went up or down, so did worker remuneration.

The sliding-scale system evoked a mixed reaction. In coalmining it was generally opposed by the miners, who saw in it a means by which the companies could erode wage rates by flooding the market with their coal. As W. J. Ashley commented in 1903: "An employer has not the same motive to hold back his stock of coal under a sliding scale — and the same is true of any plan tantamount to a sliding scale — as if wages were regulated by competition . . . when the coal owners offer to sell at reduced prices — especially when they make long contracts — they hope to reduce their labor costs."[6] The particular sliding-scale formula used in coal seemed badly designed, the chief popular objection to it being that "the confounded thing had no bottom," as one South Wales collier put it. Miners' pay was badly squeezed during the downturns of a generally declining industry. Economist Jan Tinbergen, reminiscing in his Nobel Prize lecture about early econometric forages into "the explanation of the fluctuations in the general wage index in Britain before 1900," noted that "no good fit could be obtained unless as one of the explanatory variables an index of mineral prices were included. After an intensive search I found that among the wages in various industries those for miners fluctuated by far the most and that for

some time there prevailed a sliding-scale arrangement link-
ing miners' wages directly with wholesale coal prices."[7] By
the end of the century, most mines were paying straight
wages, although this did not help to stem the sharp class
strife that always characterized the coal industry.

On the other hand, the sliding-scale system seemed to
enjoy some success in the British iron and steel industry.
Union Secretary Trow's typical reaction in 1892 was, "We
believe it would be most satisfactory if this principle were
generally adopted . . . In our experience of the past, we
have had less trouble in the period in which sliding scales
have obtained."[8] J. E. C. Munro, the leading academic student of it, enthusiastically described "the principle of the
sliding scale" in 1885 as "the greatest discovery in the distribution of wealth since Ricardo's enunciation of the law
of rent."[9] William Smart wrote about the contrast with
coalmining in 1894 that "a good sliding scale so unites the
interests of both parties as to make them realize that capital and labor make as good allies as they make bad ene-
mies."[10] Steel magnate Andrew Carnegie proclaimed, "It is
the solution of the capital and labor problem because it
makes them partners — alike in prosperity and adver-
sity."[11] The British iron and steel industry remained nota-
bly free of industrial conflict for a very long time. The
sliding scale there lasted until it got caught up in the strict
wage and price controls of the World War II era, and it
never made a comeback after that.

Here and there throughout the United States, sliding
scales or related systems were sporadically used in several
early industries with mixed success. Describing the operation of a sliding scale in the largest American textile mill at
Fall River, a 1909 *Quarterly Journal of Economics* article
stated that "the plan has brought vividly to the attention of

the manufacturers and the operatives a realization of their common interests, and has revived in a measure that sense of partnership which once existed in the earlier stages of our industrial development."[12] The original Proctor & Gamble profit-sharing plan, introduced in 1887, divided net profits between the company and its employees in the same proportion as total wages bore to the total costs of production and marketing. Each employee then received a semiannual bonus dividend proportional to the ratio of his wage to total wages. Colonel William Henry Proctor, chief architect of the plan, strongly believed that profit sharing would increase employee involvement and improve efficiency.[13]

In the American economy today, employee payment plans sometimes called "profit sharing" exist for a subset of firms, comprising more than 15 percent of the total, including such large corporations as Eastman-Kodak, Proctor & Gamble, Xerox, Sears Roebuck, Texas Instruments, Kellogg, Chase Manhattan, Bankamerica, J. C. Penney, Safeway, Standard Oil of California, and several others.[14] In these larger profit-sharing corporations the employer's contribution typically averages 5 percent to 10 percent of an employee's pay. For smaller companies the profit-sharing label is often a misnomer, at least from an economist's standpoint. The term is typically used rather loosely to describe almost any payment beyond the cash wage, often chosen at the discretion of the employer rather than spelled out in an explicit formula. Frequently "profit sharing" refers to what should more properly be called "employee stock ownership plans" (ESOPs), for example.

Federal law offers tax benefits for almost any kind of profit-sharing plan that puts the worker's share in a deferred payment fund, typically to be used for retirement purposes. Most existing profit-sharing plans do not actually share profits on a current payment basis, but are more like a pension arrangement that escapes the regulations and paperwork required for more formal retirement plans. (For example, the Employee Retirement Income Security Act limits investment in own-company stock to 10 percent of a pension plan's assets, but does not impose such restrictions on profit-sharing plans.) Of the 38 largest "profit-sharing" companies in the United States, 28 are fully deferred, 6 offer a limited kind of immediate cash option (up to half of the profit share), and only 4 hold out the possibility of full cash disbursement.

There *are* genuine immediate-cash-distribution plans with a significant share component among U.S. firms, but they are scarce. A prominent example is the Lincoln Electric Company, the world's largest manufacturer of arc-welding equipment. A $450 million company, Lincoln Electric pays its 2600 employees a year-end supplementary bonus whose value has varied over the postwar years from 70 percent to 130 percent of wages, averaging about 105 percent. The profit-sharing bonus is calculated as a residual, constituting the entirety of what remains after paying out all the obligations of the corporation, including taxes, reserves set aside for maintenance and expansion of business, and dividends to stockholders. The size of the annual bonus pool is thus determined by the company's economic performance during that year, typically amounting to between 40 percent and 55 percent of pretax, prebonus profits. Along with the bonus, Lincoln offers a Guaranteed Continuous Employment Plan, assuring that every full-time employee who has been with the company more than two years will be offered work for at least 75 percent of the standard forty-hour week. Lincoln has not had a layoff since 1951 when the Guaranteed Continuous Employment

Plan was inaugurated. There seems to be a strong emphasis on avoiding barriers between management and workers at all levels, which is uncommon in the American workplace.[15] The Lincoln pattern is duplicated among a few other U.S. profit-sharing firms, but they are rather infrequent examples.

It is difficult to draw tight inferences from such a limited sample of nonwage compensation systems. My intent has been only to show that such examples have existed before and to some extent exist now. There is nothing, I believe, in principle militating against a share system of paying labor.

No one seems to have thought much about the macroeconomic implications of alternative compensation systems.[16] The basic question is this: What happens to overall economic performance if many big firms use share contracts?

In the short run, the coefficients or parameters of a contract may be treated as fixed. But they are really only partially fixed. Over the longer run these same coefficients or parameters are changeable and will be adjusted to reflect market conditions. What differences there are between the economic effects of different contract forms will therefore tend to be limited to the short run — that period of temporary disequilibrium during which the phenomenon of involuntary unemployment manifests itself.

Before going on to analyze the macroeconomic implications of alternative compensation systems, I must first clarify what is meant by a share system and how it differs from a wage system. In a share system a worker's compensation is directly and automatically adjusted by some index of the firm's well-being, such as profits per worker or product price. In a wage system, the worker's compensation is not directly tied to any such firm-specific index; typically it is expressed in money terms, although it might be adjusted by an economy-wide indicator such as the consumer price index.

There is a subtlety here which turns out to be crucially important. It was shown in Chapter 2 that, for a given demand schedule, such firm-specific indices as product price, revenue per worker, or profit per worker are inversely proportional to the amount of labor the firm hires. So any remuneration formula linked to these indexes is also inversely proportional to the amount of labor hired.

The analytic essence of a share contract is that if workers are laid off or quit, the remaining employees are paid more, whereas if new workers are hired, all employees are paid less. Of course the mechanism by which this comes about is indirect and may well escape detection in the sea of uncertainty surrounding a firm's well-being. But it is nevertheless always lurking in the background of a share system, and its implications are very important. If a firm hires more workers, they produce more output. Other things being equal, if not immediately then gradually, that will tend to depress price, lower revenue per worker, and decrease profit per worker. When some part of a worker's pay depends upon these firm-specific indices, taking on more workers by the firm will have a tendency (if everything else could be held constant) to lower pay. Conversely, laying off some workers will have a tendency under a share contract to raise the level of compensation.

These are strictly short-run consequences of a share contract, which hold only so long as it is in effect. Over the longer run such tendencies must be modified, at least in a full-employment environment. When the contract is next revised, the coefficients or parameters being used to determine worker remuneration will change more nearly to equalize rates of pay throughout the economy. (Otherwise the lower-paying firms will lose workers over time to their higher-paying neighbors.) But in the short run, when the contract is made, a share system means that worker remuneration automatically increases as more labor is laid off and declines as more labor is hired. In a wage system, by contrast, an employed worker's pay is not directly affected by the hiring or firing of labor.

A share contract, then, can generally be defined as any payment mechanism where, throughout the life of the contract, worker remuneration varies inversely with the firm's employment level, all other things being held constant. Actually, by this abstract definition, many semiartificial formulas that do not depend on the well-being of the firm, and therefore do not rely on uncertain elements like the state of demand, qualify as "share contracts." Suppose, for example, a firm agrees to pay a fixed total wage bill over some specified period. No matter how many workers are hired, or what condition it is in, throughout that period the firm will pay out to labor a certain fixed total amount. Instead of paying $24 per hour and then choosing to hire 500,000 workers, GM commits itself in advance to paying a total of $12 million per hour to be shared among all its workers over the life of the contract. (This kind of payment scheme was called the "wages fund doctrine" by a number of classical economists, including John Stuart Mill, who believed it to be a true description of how an economy as a whole operates.) The fixed wage bill is a share contract because, if the firm wishes to lay off 1 percent of its workers in the short run, the remaining workers get an immediate 1 percent pay raise. (There are any number of variations on this theme. For example, a share contract might specify the base wage for a certain target employment level but alter it by, say, .25 percent for every 1 percent change in the employment level from target.)

To summarize: under a share contract, worker compensation is tied to a formula that makes it vary inversely with the firm's level of employment. Under a wage contract, worker compensation is independent of the firm's employment level.

Here is another way of seeing the difference. Under a wage contract, the average cost of labor to the firm (what each worker is paid) is constant and therefore *equals* the marginal cost of hiring one additional unit of labor. Under a share contract, the marginal cost of labor is strictly *less* than the average cost of labor. When an extra worker is hired on a share contract, that very slightly depresses the pay (or average cost) of every other worker on the same contract. Whenever the average cost of labor declines as more labor is hired, it must mean that marginal cost is below average cost (just as average revenue, or price, declining with volume of output must mean that marginal revenue is below average revenue). There is simply no way worker compensation can vary inversely with the level of employment unless the extra cost to the firm of hiring one more worker is less than the average cost, or pay, of all the other workers. Only if the last increment of labor cost is less than the average of all preceeding increments will the average be pulled down when one more worker is hired.

Consider the wage-bill contract, under whose terms the firm agrees to pay throughout some period a fixed total amount to its labor force regardless of the employment level. (In this example the total wage bill is a quasi-fixed "compensation parameter" during the short run, although it can be changed over the longer run.) The average cost of labor (the share each worker receives) is just the wage bill divided by the number of employees; hence it declines as the employment level increases. But the marginal cost of labor to the firm is zero, because the firm's labor budget is fixed in the short run and each additional employee costs no more.

Or consider again the hypothetical General Motors revenue-sharing plan of Chapter 1. When each worker was paid a straight wage (including benefits) of $24 per hour, the average *and* marginal cost of labor to the firm were both $24 per hour. That also represented, in a profit-maximizing state, the extra net revenue that an additional labor hour creates, or the marginal value of labor to the firm. The average revenue per labor hour was $36 by assumption. Suppose, as in the example, that the UAW and GM agree instead to pay each worker a two-thirds share of GM's average revenue per worker over some contract period. (The share coefficient 2/3 is a quasi-fixed compensation parameter in this example, constant during the short run but flexible over the longer run.) The average cost of labor remains $24 per hour. But the marginal cost of an extra unit of labor to GM is two-thirds of the increase in the revenue pie created by one extra labor hour, or $16.

I could go on. Sharecropping in Indian agriculture, the sliding scale of the British iron and steel industry, the constant wages fund of the classical economists, the Japanese system of profit sharing, or a mixture of a money-wage floor plus a fraction of company sales per worker — all represent examples of share contracts where, at any given time, the marginal cost of labor to the employer is less than the average cost.

Any system where a substantial number of big firms are

operating with the marginal cost of labor lower than the average cost of labor will have an inherent predilection toward providing more employment and expanding output. The trend may be disguised, but it is nonetheless difficult to thwart over time. To see this tendency clearly, imagine the following scenario. Suppose a wage economy is stagnating in a low-employment trap, as described toward the end of Chapter 4. Each firm is operating at a point of maximum profit, but the economy is caught in a vicious circle where insufficient demand causes high unemployment and low purchasing power, which then feeds back to reinforce the insufficient demand. The condition might be corrected in the long run by wage changes or other adjustments, but for the near term the economy is stuck in an unemployment state.

Now let the following thought experiment be performed. Suppose that a fair number (say more than 500) of the big firms suddenly change to a share system. Suppose further that the compensation parameters of each firm's new share contract are precisely set so that the initial money value of the income per worker now paid (at the previous employment level) exactly equals the old wage. For the sake of concreteness, imagine that the firms go over to a revenue-sharing contract, although the arguments generalize to any share contract.

Under the wage contract, labor was hired to the point where its marginal value to the firm just equaled the wage, which represents the average and marginal cost of labor. After conversion to an equivalent share contract, the average cost of labor (each worker's compensation) is the same. But the marginal cost of labor under the share contract is now lower than the average cost. Hence the marginal value of an extra unit of labor to the firm now exceeds its marginal cost. If there is available unemployed labor, each share firm will attempt to expand.

Were just one firm alone to convert from a wage contract to an equivalent share contract (initially paying the same compensation), that firm would increase employment and output, lowering its price, lowering its revenue per worker, and decreasing the pay of each worker. But if all firms (or a significant number) convert to a share system, something like a balanced expansion of the economy would take place, with the increased demand from higher spending of newly employed workers feeding back to keep prices, revenues per worker, and labor remuneration more or less steady but with the economy automatically going toward a higher employment level.

The expansion of a share system ends when there is no more unemployment. At that point each share firm wishes to expand further, but it cannot because there is no more unemployed labor to be found.

A more realistic description of how a share system would actually operate might be slightly less crisp than the above, but it should not be very different in principle. There might be somewhat less alacrity to the search for new workers, but the general inclinations of the labor-absorption process should remain. In the real world, price setting has some built-in sluggishness (although nothing compared to wages), there are decision lags and noninstantaneous adjustments of all sorts, labor is imperfectly mobile (having monopolistic elements in some situations but monopsonistic features in others), the exact specification of the macroeconomic (particularly monetary) transmission mechanism will play some role, and so forth. Yet these and other elaborations can be accommodated in the basic model without changing its essential structure or the fundamental conclusions.

However much disguised by institutional inertias or buffeted by the momentary forces of change and uncertainty, a share system possesses a relentless underlying drive toward absorbing unemployed workers, increasing output, and lowering prices which does not cease until all available labor is fully employed. Even then the share engine attempts to push farther in the same direction by spinning its wheels on the icy perimeter of full employment, primed to lurch forward the instant that traction is provided by spreading the grit of fresh labor.

Toward what configuration does a share economy tend in a stationary environment of slow changes? The somewhat reassuring answer, admittedly given at a high level of abstraction, is that both a wage system and any form of share system incline toward exactly the same long-run equilibrium. A visitor from Mars could not tell the difference between two undisturbed economies that were alike in all respects except that one was a wage system and the other a share system. In both systems managers would manage — on behalf of stockholders — and workers would work; the workers would be paid the same real dollar amounts for the same levels of ability, skill, training, and effort; essentially the same issues concerning to what degree individual pay formulas should be modified by a piece-rate factor or by a length-of-service factor arise in both systems and would be resolved similarly; the rate of return on capital would be equivalent; machines would substitute for labor to the identical degree; airplanes would be made of equal materials; people would not be clothed differently; washing machines would be indistinguishable; and the beer would taste alike. The same long-run forces would determine the same resource-allocation patterns, independent of the compensation system.

The reason is that in the very long run—abstracting away from unemployment, from shocks or disturbances, and from the fact that a disequilibrium path ultimately affects an equilibrium position—essentially the same invisible hand guides both wage and share systems. The only difference is that the labor-payment formulas and parameters *look* different in the two systems.

 But while the labor-payment formulas might look different, in fact they must be doing the same thing in equilibrium. Over a long enough time interval, compensation parameters are flexible and will be adjusted under competitive pressure to yield the same compensation to workers of the same skill level, equal to their common marginal value to the firms. If workers of identical quality are not paid the same, they will migrate from low-paying to high-paying firms. Given the fact that in equilibrium every firm must end up paying the prevailing labor compensation anyway, a share firm can do no better than to hire labor to the point where the marginal value of the extra worker is equal to the prevailing remuneration, setting its share parameters accommodatingly to yield the going compensation.

Thus the fundamental rules of resource allocation are the same under wage and share systems *in long-run equilibrium*, and the three major decisions of the firm are identically resolved. The share firm in equilibrium can only obtain labor at the competitive rate prevailing throughout the rest of the economy. That being the case, the best the share firm can do in the long run is to hire labor to the point where its marginal value equals the prevailing pay; the share parameters are then passively set during contract time almost as an afterthought to yield the prevailing pay at the firm's desired employment level.

The theoretical isomorphism between wage and share systems is not only limited to static situations where the stock of capital is given. Essentially the same logic applies to establishing the stock of capital itself over longer periods across which it can be treated as variable. It is true that, if pay parameters were permanently frozen, then capitalists in a share system would underinvest relative to a wage system because any incremental output would have to be shared with labor. But this is strictly a short-term effect, which does not hold over a longer time frame when compensation coefficients can be flexible and are basically determined by competitive forces. In the long run the prevailing pay level represents the term of trade between labor and a dollar's worth of any factor that substitutes for it. In all compensation systems, that will induce a volume of investment to the point where the long-run marginal rate of substitution between an extra dollar's worth of durable capital and an extra dollar's worth of labor designed to work with it is equal to one. At the appropriate level of abstraction, then, share and wage systems stimulate equal efforts toward output-increasing improvements.

Although share and wage systems have identical resource-allocation patterns in stationary equilibrium, there is a marked difference in the degree of tension of their respective labor markets. The wage system has supply *equal* to demand in the labor market. A wage firm wants to hire exactly as much labor as it is hiring under its current wage contract. But the share system has demand for labor *greater* than supply of labor. A share firm always wants to hire more labor than it is actually able to hire by the profit-maximizing contract parameters that it has itself selected.

The contrast can be seen very clearly for the case of sharecropping, abstracted from risk and incentive effects. If agriculture is worked on a wage system, there is but a limited appetite for labor. The landowner chooses to hire workers only to the point where the marginal value of an extra worker's product equals the prevailing wage. But in a sharecropping system, it is the workers who choose where they should be allocated. The owner whose land is being cropped is always hungry for more labor. The more croppers working the land, the bigger is the output pie — and the slice going to the landowner. The sharecroppers will allocate themselves to the point where the money value of each worker's share is equal to the prevailing level of pay. Given that this is to be so, the landowner can do no better than to take on labor to the point where the difference between the value of output and the total remuneration to labor at the going rate is maximized, then passively setting the share parameter to yield that going pay needed to attract the croppers at the desired level of employment. It is as if the share landowner's profit-maximizing problem were split into two almost separate subproblems. The first subproblem is solved as if a straight wage were being paid at the prevailing level; the second is solved when the share parameter is mechanically chosen to yield the prevailing pay once the optimal levels of employment and output have been determined. In the equilibrium states of both share and wage systems, labor is therefore worked to the point where its marginal value equals the prevailing pay. But at the parameter values selected to bring about this profit-maximizing condition, the share landowner always wishes to obtain more labor on the margin; the wage landowner is content with exactly the current level.

Transactions in the labor market of a share system are strictly constrained on the supply side, just as the product market of a monopolistically competitive economy is demand-constrained. So there is a crude but important analogy here. Very roughly speaking, the wage system is to the share system as perfect competition is to monopolistic competition.

When average revenue (price) does not change with the level of output, we have the case of perfect competition, and it results in a product-market equilibrium where supply equals demand. When the average cost of labor (the compensation to labor) does not change with employment, we have the wage system; it yields a labor-market equilibrium where supply also equals demand. In both instances the systems settle into what might be called states of neutral equilibrium.

But when average revenue (price) declines with output, which is the case of monopolistic competition, the resulting equilibrium has supply greater than demand, so that the product market is constantly under pressure. And when the average cost of labor (its pay) varies inversely with employment — the share system — the equilibrium demand for labor exceeds the supply, and the labor market is in what might be called a state of suction.

The possible combinations of product-market and labor-market configurations are illustrated in the accompanying diagram.

Just as the monopolistically competitive firm is very keen to supply more of its product to any potential customer, so the share firm is eager and willing to hire more labor at any time. There is at least one important distinction, though. While the status of a product market (compet-

	PERFECT COMPETITION	MONOPOLISTIC COMPETITION
WAGE SYSTEM	Indifferent Seller of Product — Indifferent Buyer of Labor	Eager to Sell More Product — Indifferent Buyer of Labor
SHARE SYSTEM	Indifferent Seller of Product — Eager to Buy More Labor	Eager to Sell More Product — Eager to Buy More Labor

The Firm's Attitude Toward Its Markets

itive or monopolistic) must pretty much be treated as a given datum, depending on the elasticity of the relevant demand function, a labor payment system is more deeply a matter of human discretion. As a society we have the option of choosing (or at least influencing) the mode in which labor is to be compensated in the short run, if that is deemed important.

8
Life in a Share Economy

THE REAL PATTERN OF RE-source allocation concerns what is produced, how it is produced, and for whom it is produced. The long-run allocation pattern toward which the economy tends, abstracting away from shocks or other immediate interferences, is independent of the compensation system. If the world were completely unchanging or stationary, there would be no discernible difference between a wage system and a share system.

But our world is not in equilibrium. Like a planet engulfed in a meteor swarm, the economy is continually being peppered by unpredicted disturbances. The important issue concerns how an economic system performs when it is hit by unforeseen shocks. And here a share economy *is* different from a wage economy because it has much more resilient disequilibrium properties.

The wage economy has only a vague long-run tendency to drift toward full employment, as wages and other sticky parameters are gradually adjusted by the invisible hand. But conditions rarely last long enough to let it stay there. At any given time a wage economy will find itself at full employment only, so to speak, by accident. The invisible hand moves far too slowly.

The share system, however, has a strong built-in mechanism that automatically stabilizes the economy at full employment, even before the long-run tendencies have had a chance to assert their dominance. A wage economy has only the weak corrective force of the invisible hand slowly changing sticky parameters over time. But a share economy has the direct "strong force" of positive excess demand for labor (as well as the indirect "weak force" of eventual parameter changes) pulling it toward full employment. Even if the wrong share parameters prevail, the strong force of the share system will maintain full employment. By contrast, a wage that is too high relative to aggregate demand (or, as it is more usually expressed, aggregate demand that is too low relative to the wage rate) will induce unemployment in a wage system.

In long-run equilibrium the compensation mode of any payment system is but an inessential appendage to the real economy — like a dog's tail. But in the short run, the sticky compensation parameter of a particular payment mode becomes the tail that wags the dog.

To see clearly just how different are the disequilibrium properties of wage and share systems, perform the following thought experiment. Start with two identical-twin wage and share economies in long-run stationary equilibrium. The economies are exactly alike except that one is a share system while the other pays wages. Then disturb the equilibrium by an unanticipated shock, and see how the twins react.[1] The prototypical test for disequilibrium properties is to throw an extra worker on the job market and to observe how the system reacts. Strictly speaking, when a new person unexpectedly enters the labor market, a disequilibrium situation is created.

The immediate profit-maximizing response of the share firm is to eagerly offer employment because the marginal value of the new worker exceeds the marginal cost. After soaking up all involuntarily unemployed workers, a share system will eventually adjust compensation parameter values to reestablish long-run equilibrium. The point is that the unemployed worker is absorbed right away and immediately starts producing goods and services, without having to wait for the outcome of what may be a difficult adjustment process.

By contrast, in the stationary state of a wage system the marginal value of labor already equals its marginal cost, and the firm is not interested in hiring any more workers. There is no automatic short-run tendency to absorb unemployed workers into a system where compensation is rigidly indexed to money, to a representative basket of consumer goods, or to any other *numeraire* whose value does not decline as the firm hires more labor. Only a complicated, roundabout, and extremely problematical adjustment of wages, which succeeds in lowering real labor costs relative to product demand, will cause a wage system to absorb unemployed workers.

A share system looks very much like a labor-shortage economy. Share firms ever hungry for labor are always on the prowl—cruising around like vacuum cleaners on wheels, searching in nooks and crannies for extra workers to pull in at existing compensation parameter values. Such an economy inherently resists recession. Every share firm wants to hire more workers at the equilibrium parameter rates, making temporary additional profits by absorbing any incipient pockets of unemployment that arise or can be found. The profits from assimilating a new source of unemployed workers are temporary, because in the long run they will eventually be squeezed out by rising compensation parameter rates and by workers transferring to other firms. But the mere fact that such profits turn out to be transitory does not make them any less real to the firm that manages to capture them. This kind of "suction" equilibrium, in which all firms are actively seeking to employ more workers at existing compensation parameter rates, is strikingly different from the zero demand for unemployed labor under a wage system.

Unlike perfect competition, modern industrial capitalism is a system characterized by a more or less permanent excess supply of goods. As we have noted, monopolistically competitive firms are aggressive in product markets, forever eager to find new customers and to sell more output at existing prices. The thesis of this book is that the ultimate solution to stagflationist tendencies involves redesigning incentives so that firms are equally aggressive on the factor-market side in the analogous sense of having permanent job vacancies they are always striving to fill.

The analysis of more complicated shocks is like the example of a pure change in labor supply. In each case the central feature is the same. A share economy has demand for labor strictly greater than supply and remains at a level of positive excess demand even after undergoing a small disequilibrating shock. A wage economy has demand for labor equal to supply and therefore tends not to absorb unemployed workers after a disturbance.

Consider, for example, how a share system automatically cushions first-round contractionary demand shocks, even before existing compensation parameter rates can be changed. Suppose the demand for a firm's output declines. The share firm will react to a moderate decline in demand by trying to retain workers and keep up production, maintaining volume by lowering output price. Workers may choose to quit if their pay is diminished below what could be obtained elsewhere, but they are never deliberately fired. Only if the decline in demand is sufficiently acute in one sector to overcome the positive excess demand for labor will firms choose to lay off workers. But in principle any newly unemployed workers can find jobs in the less severely afflicted sectors of the economy which continue to want more labor. The basic point is that the positive excess demand for unemployed labor in the share system as a whole provides a safety margin for automatically reacting to changed conditions by maintaining full employment even out of equilibrium. The wage firm, on the other hand, reacts to a decline in demand by decreasing output and employment, with ambiguous effects on price; for example, as we saw in Chapter 2, price is unchanged in the standard base case of constant marginal cost and a constant elasticity of demand. In both systems, long-run equilibrium is reestablished only after a complicated adjustment of compensation parameters and a reallocation of workers throughout the economy. But the share system does not disemploy workers or otherwise interfere with the productive flow of output during the interim.

Consider again the highly idealized GM-UAW scenario. The marginal revenue created by an extra hour of labor is

$24, equal to what the workers are paid (including benefits). The average revenue per hour of labor is $36. The markup coefficient is 1.5 ($36/$24), which implies a long-run demand elasticity of 3. Output is assumed to be proportional to labor. To give the story a slightly more realistic flavor, this time I will assume that the labor contract is of a more practical "hybrid" share form: workers are paid a base wage of $16 per hour plus a revenue-sharing bonus calculated as 2/9 (22.2 percent) of GM revenues per worker. (The bonus comes to $8 [2/9 × $36] in the example.) This is mathematically equivalent to a profit-sharing system paying a base wage of $20.57 per hour plus a 2/9 share of "gross operating profit" per worker. (For the purposes of this example, gross operating profits per worker is equal to revenue per worker [$36 per hour] minus labor cost per worker [$20.57].) Needless to say, these numerical assumptions are being made more for the sake of expository convenience than factual accuracy. Other specifications would yield similar qualitative conclusions.

At the current full-employment equilibrium, the marginal value of labor to GM is $24 per worker-hour. But the marginal cost of hiring an extra hour of labor is only $18.67 ($16 + 2/9 × $24). Every extra worker hired on the current share contract is worth $5.33 ($24 − $18.67) per hour to GM. Under the share contract, therefore, GM equilibrates in a state of excess demand for labor. Why, then, does the company not attempt to compete actively for more labor by bidding up its pay?

Suppose GM did try to bid away labor from other firms, by raising the base wage by a dollar — from $16 to $17 per hour. (A similar analysis would follow if the share parameter were bid up, say from 2/9 to 1/4.) When the economy-wide prevailing pay for the skill level of an automobile assembly worker is $24 per hour, GM will now be able to lure workers away from other companies since it is currently paying $25 per hour. The newly hired workers produce more automobiles, driving down the price per auto and the revenue per worker. New workers will continue to join GM until the revenue per worker has eventually declined by 12.5 percent from $36 to $31.50, at which point a competitive pay level of $24 ($17 + ⅔ × $31.50) has been restored. Yet now GM is actually making less profits than before. Previously the marginal value of labor was $24 per worker-hour. Now revenue per worker-hour has been lowered by $4.50, which implies the same proportional decline of 12.5 percent in the marginal revenue product of labor to $21 per worker-hour. Given the prevailing pay of $24 per hour, GM is no longer in a profit-maximizing position, having hired workers to the point where they are worth $21 per hour on the margin. After this experiment the company has succeeded in attracting more labor, but now it wishes it hadn't performed the trial because total profits are lower. The resolution of the seeming paradox is that while GM desires more labor on the *old* contract, it will be made worse off if it tries to issue a *new* contract with higher pay parameters. So sooner or later, by trial and error, GM will settle back on a base wage of $16 per hour along with a revenue-sharing coefficient of ⅔.

Now suppose GM alone is hit with a 10 percent decline in demand while the rest of the economy remains unchanged. Under a wage system, GM management's profit-maximizing response is to maintain the price of automobiles but to cut back production by 10 percent and to lay off 10 percent of its work force. The profit-maximizing reaction under the hybrid share system is to maintain full production and full employment by rolling automobile prices back 3⅓ percent (the 10 percent decline in demand divided by the price elasticity of 3). GM revenues then also fall by 3⅓ percent, so each worker's pay is cut by 27¢ per hour, from $24 ($16 + 2/9 × $36) to $23.73 ($16 + 2/9 × $36 × 96⅔ percent). The UAW is therefore buying a 10 percent saving of GM jobs for a 1.1 percent pay cut (27¢/$24). Even after a 10 percent decline in demand, GM's profit-maximizing strategy under the share contract is to maintain full employment. This is because the marginal value produced by an extra worker is $23.20 per hour (96⅔ percent × $24), whereas the marginal cost of an extra labor hour is only $21.16 ($16 + 2/9 × $23.20).

In its initial equilibrium state, GM's total revenues were $18 million per hour ($36 × 500,000 workers), while total labor costs were $12 million per hour ($24 × 500,000). After the 10 percent reduction in demand, the total money paid out to labor under the wage contract is $10.8 million per hour ($24 × 500,000 × 90 percent), whereas the total money paid out to labor under the share contract is $11.865 million per hour ($23.73 × 500,000). Thus GM workers *as a group* take home 9.9 percent more pay under the share contract than under the wage contract, although the high-seniority UAW members who already have job security sustain a 1.1 percent pay cut. (Note that the original pool of GM workers would not fare better *as a group* under a share contract if GM were able suddenly to hire a lot more outside labor and thereby significantly dilute every GM worker's pay.)

Now look at GM's side of the ledger after the contractionary shock. Under the wage contract, revenues have declined by 10 percent, from $18 million to $16.2 million per hour. With the share contract, revenues decrease by 3⅓ percent, to $17.4 million per hour. So GM's gross operating profits decline from $6 million per hour ($18 − $12) to $5.4 million per hour under the wage contract ($16.2 − $10.8), while they only fall to $5.535 million per hour under the share contract ($17.4 − $11.865). Both GM and the UAW withstand a decline in demand better under a share contract. Although this is only a numerical example, its basic feature can be generalized. Because of a bigger output pie, higher total labor payments in a share system are compatible with higher profits.

→   The share-contract example does not end where it was left. After the 10 percent decline of demand, GM is in a state of disequilibrium. The marginal value of a worker to the firm ($23.20) is less than the economy-wide prevailing pay ($24), which means a basic equilibrium condition is being violated. Long-run equilibrium is reattained as follows. When the prevailing pay throughout the economy for the skill level of an automobile assembly worker is $24 per hour, GM will not be able to hold on to its work force (even though it wants to) while paying only $23.73. Above-usual labor turnover will be experienced as marginal workers turn down GM job offers in favor of better-paying opportunities elsewhere, and it becomes more difficult to replace retirees. The net emigration of GM workers will drive up pay at GM by itself, since the revenue per worker will automatically increase with fewer workers. Unless automobile revenues recover, the next time a contract is negotiated the UAW is going to put on some pressure for the pay level to be brought back up to the competitive norm of $24 per hour — by raising the base wage component from $16 to $16.27, or by increasing the revenue-sharing coefficient from 22.2 percent to 23.1 percent. If such measures are not taken, GM will continue to lose workers until the revenue per employee increases enough to compensate remaining workers at the going rate of $24 per hour.

One way or the other, GM will not be able to keep on indefinitely paying its workers below the going market rate. If demand for GM cars remains depressed, say because the buying public has permanently turned toward other automakers' products, the long-run adjustment of both wage and share systems will identically require GM to hire 10 percent fewer workers and produce 10 percent less automobiles (that is, until the point where the net marginal value of an extra worker equals the competitive pay of $24 per hour). But a share system manages this transition far better than a wage system, without taking jobs away from workers in the interim.

Both systems respond to shifts in relative demand by sending a signal that eventually transfers workers out of a losing firm or sector and over to a winner. Under a wage system the signal to a worker that his firm is a loser in the game of capitalist roulette — and it is time to look for a new job with a winning firm — is that the worker is laid off. The corresponding signal under a share system is that the worker's compensation is lowered. (Or, more realistically, it does not keep pace, as pay elsewhere does, with productivity advances.)

Note that it is not the automatic pay cut per se which drives the whole example. If pay were lowered by 1.1 percent on a straight wage contract, that would only save 3.3 percent of GM jobs (a 1.1 percent wage or price change times a demand elasticity of 3), a far cry from the 10 percent actually saved. It is not difficult to construct situations that emphasize this point even more dramatically. Under a fixed wage-bill type of share contract, for example, pay is not automatically lowered after a decline in demand, and yet the firm chooses to retain all its workers.

Thus the share system does not eliminate unemployment by in effect lowering wages to the point where equilibrium is automatically maintained. The driving force behind full employment in a share system is not the *actual* lowering of pay during a recessionary shock, but rather the *potential* lowering that would occur if more workers could be hired. (This is what drives a wedge between marginal and average costs of labor.) So long as enough firms use share contracts, there will be no free-floating unemployed labor available for a particular share firm to hire at potentially decreased pay; thus no worker's compensation will actually be lowered by the direct effect of a firm's hiring "too much" labor after a general contractionary shock.

Both wage and share systems naturally exhibit some friction or inflexibility of contract parameters. In principle, a share system is no less disequilibrated by shocks than is a wage system. The point is not that one system operates closer to equilibrium than another, but rather that the form of disequilibrium response is different. Roughly speaking, the short-term response of a share economy holds the quantity of hired labor (and output) at its full-employment level, with the disequilibrium showing itself on the price (or value) side (workers are temporarily not paid their marginal value). Wage economies, on the other hand, tend to respond to contractionary shocks by holding equilibrium prices (or values) in line (workers are always compensated their marginal value) while the quantities of employment (and output) decline. In the long run both systems tend to the same equilibrium, but their short-run behavior is quite different.[2] Although there is an abstract symmetry between price and quantity adjustment modes, only a pedant would be indifferent to them in practice. It is far more important for overall economic welfare that the system as a whole maintains a full-employment flow of goods and services throughout a contractionary shock than that some marginal-value conditions on the level of the firm are being satisfied.

Generally speaking, the size of deflationary shock that can be absorbed by the economy without causing unemployment depends on the number of share firms and the strength of each share firm's feedback loop connecting higher employment back to lower unit labor costs. In that sense, a compensation scheme has more desirable macroeconomic properties when the share component is large relative to the wage component, and there is a significant degree of excess demand for labor by the firm. If the fraction of all monopolistically competitive big firms covered by meaningful share contracts is sufficiently high relative to the unemployment rate, the share firms should be able to lead the rest of the economy out of a recession.

By eliminating unemployment, a share system makes the typical worker better off and pays out more income to labor as a whole. It is true that the tenured, high-seniority worker who already has job security with a wage contract may now face some immediate variability in pay. (This depends on the particular form of the share contract.) But, on average, the high-seniority worker will also earn more in a share system because full employment and a greater division of labor generally mean more output, greater income, and brisk demand. And a great deal of the variability we now observe in the demand for a firm's product will be removed because the macroeconomy is much more stable when it is permanently operating at full capacity.

Like free trade, a share system is highly beneficial to the population as a whole. The vast bulk of the working class benefits from aggregate output being produced, and consumed, at the full-employment level. But, as when a protective tariff is removed from an industry, not every single person is made better off by an uncompensated transition to a share economy. The biggest *relative* loser in converting to a share system is the tenured, high-seniority worker who receives, in a handful of overpaid industries, a noncompetitive wage above the natural age-profile rate for that skill and experience level. Such a privileged worker will not lose his job under a share contract, but he cannot hope to indefinitely continue being paid more than the going rate that others in a comparable position elsewhere are receiving for similar work. Rather, management with a share contract will simply offset, over time, such fabricated levels of pay by taking on additional workers, thereby driving down individual share income. While friends and relations will likely benefit greatly from conversion to a share system (since they will now readily find work where it was previously scarce), the artificially privileged worker will lose the "tariff" premium above competitive pay scales, unless length of company service is explicitly included as a pay-adjustment factor in the share contract.

Any profit-maximizing firm whose marginal value of labor is higher than the marginal cost of labor will seek to employ more workers if it can. But wouldn't the senior workers of a share firm resent and try to resist the new workers coming on board who, in effect, lower the pay of all the employees? In addressing this issue we must first of all distinguish between abstract economic properties, however important, and readily observable things. When an entire economy of share firms is geared up and functioning smoothly, there is a significant excess demand for labor as a whole and there are no long-term jobless people to be picked up easily. New labor must come primarily from other share firms, presumably yielded up in grudging amounts. In that environment, the tenuous aftermath of hiring some more workers in one firm will scarcely be noticed, disguised as it must be behind a myriad of seemingly more important economic changes that directly influence the income of an individual firm. Besides, even should the subtle connection be made, it becomes an issue only when the senior workers are trying to protect a noncompetitive pay level held artificially above the going market rate for that job category — new workers will have no incentive to join the firm in the first place unless they can receive a higher pay there than elsewhere.

A share system can be the centerpiece of a program of prosperity for working people. Once its basic principles are adopted, however, the system springs to life and seemingly takes on its own philosophy in almost forcing labor to accept a perspective broader than wage militancy for the benefit of one particular subgroup at the expense of others. The new rules of the game say that everyone will be able to find a job at the going rate. But, to put it bluntly, workers in a share firm simply cannot expect over the long run to be continually paid above the competitive rate for their skill and experience level — the firm will naturally try to offset that possibility by drawing in more labor.

The bargaining power of labor unions is not a natural right. As a matter of fact, throughout labor history in Great Britain and the United States until well into the present century, common-law doctrine held labor unions to be an illegal "conspiracy in restraint of trade." The right of labor to bargain collectively was granted by the state, presumably to improve the welfare of the average working man and woman, only relatively recently as such things go, after years of hard-fought struggle by legions of courageous, downtrodden, underprivileged people seeking work with dignity. In its heroic era the labor movement vehemently protested against privileged classes who erected all sorts of artificial barriers to block disadvantaged outsiders from advancing. The unionized workers of today who inherit the fruits of that legacy have no legal permission to exclude or impede the open recruitment of new members and apprentices. The closed shop, which requires that firms hire only workers who are already union members, is illegal in the United States today. Under existing labor law, once a collective-bargaining agreement has been reached in a union shop, the firm is free to choose and hire new nonunion workers, all of whom must be admitted to union membership within a specified time period. In law and in custom, hiring new workers is a management prerogative, not a mandatory subject to bargaining. This is a doctrine the public can legitimately insist upon as a quid pro quo for the rights and privileges granted to labor unions by federal legislation. The share system is a better game than the wage system, but played with strict rules; and one of them is that new workers are welcome to join a share firm.

The spell of the wage system is the illusion that the welfare of a firm's employees is independent of the economic condition of the employer. Although less than one in five American workers currently belongs to a union, the labor movement as a whole has nevertheless greatly increased in workers' eyes the wage system's aura of independence from the capitalist. This dangerous delusion ignores the unemployment that it causes. And it obscures the fact that one claimant's share can only be increased to another's detriment: an environment is created where it is natural to make, and concede, incompatible claims, thus leading to the tragically self-defeating struggle for income shares that culminates in cost-push inflation. The share system, by contrast, only makes explicit what is already inherently true in a capitalist market economy — namely that the worker gets but a part of the product and, for better or worse, ultimately depends on the capitalist for employment and income, just as the capitalist depends on the worker for profits.

So the working class faces a choice. The traditional wage system offers a fixed nominal compensation for a majority who have work, but no guarantee of full employment and a raw deal for the minority without work. A share system offers full employment to all at a variable pay that may, if it is linked to company revenues or profits, fluctuate somewhat with firm-specific changes in the relative composition of demand, but is higher on average than the wage system's fixed compensation. If a particular industry is declining, so that pay rates there go down, plenty of well-paying jobs are always available elsewhere in a share economy.

What about the inflation side of stagflation in a share economy? To the extent that a share system helps to absorb unemployed labor in any way, it automatically gives the government more freedom to stabilize the value of money without having to worry so much about the adverse consequences for employment. This is a significant anti-inflationary effect by itself. But there are also direct reasons for believing that a share economy should have less of an inflationary bias than a wage economy.

Any firm whose unit labor costs are inversely related to its employment and output levels is also a firm whose labor costs in effect vary directly with the price of its output (because output and price are inversely related). The share firm must therefore act as if it has indexed its workers' pay directly to the price of its output. And an economy of share firms, each of whose labor costs are in effect indexed to their own product prices, is inherently biased against inflation because it is costly to the firms to raise prices. Other things being equal, there is less tendency for a share producer to raise prices and more tendency to lower them in response to any given shock, since all price changes now automatically show up also on the cost side.

As an example, consider the direct first-round effects of a supply-side shock which increases the cost of some raw material complementary with labor (say imported oil). The profit-maximizing wage firm will respond in the usual way by laying off workers, decreasing output, and raising price. The profit-maximizing share firm, whose demand for labor exceeds what is being supplied to it, has no wish to disemploy labor. Instead, it will react by trying to hold the same levels of employment, output, and price. The long-run adjustment of both systems is identical, involving basic changes in compensation parameters, relative prices, living standards, and resource-allocation patterns. But in the short run a share firm tries to absorb supply-side shocks without raising prices or causing unemployment.

Look at the GM example once more. The worker is paid at the prevailing competitive rate of $24 per hour, which also represents the marginal value created by an extra hour of labor. The average revenue is $36 per worker-hour. The underlying demand elasticity is 3, consistent with a markup coefficient of 1.5. Output is assumed proportional to labor employed. The share contract includes a base wage of $16 and a bonus of ⅔ of revenues per worker. Suppose a supply-side shock hits. The price of imported aluminum goes up, raising GM's costs by, say, the equivalent of 50¢ per worker-hour.

Under the wage system, the effect on GM would be as if the base wage for labor had been increased by 50¢ per hour or 2.1 percent (50¢/$24). According to the constant-markup-coefficient formula, the profit-maximizing response would then be to pass on the cost increase to the buyer by raising the price of automobiles the same 2.1 percent. (For expositional simplicity I assume that materials costs were previously negligible.) Output and employment in turn must be cut back by 6.3 percent (2.1 percent times the price elasticity of 3) to support the increased price.

The profit-maximizing response under the share contract is to maintain the same output, employment, price, and pay as before the increase in the price of aluminum. This is because the net marginal value of an extra hour of labor is $23.50 ($24 minus 50¢ for the aluminum increase), but the marginal cost of an extra hour of labor is only $21.33 ($16 + ⅔ × $24). (Note that the story would be essentially the same if there were profit sharing instead of revenue sharing, the only difference being that pay would automatically decline slightly because profits are directly depressed by an increase in the price of aluminum while revenues remain the same.)

Of course this is only an immediate response. If the aluminum price hike is permanent, then in the longer run, at a time when share-contract parameters (the $16 base wage and the ⅔ share of revenues per worker) can be renegotiated, GM will seek to lower them. Eventually the same kind of adjustment will occur as under the wage system: if pay remains at the competitive level of $24, output and employment must contract by 6.3 percent and the price of automobiles must be raised 2.1 percent so that the basic long-run equilibrium condition will again be fulfilled — the net marginal value produced by an extra worker (when aluminum costs 50¢ more per worker-hour) equals the competitive pay of $24. The eventual revenue per worker will then be $36.76 ($36 × 102.1 percent), so that if, for example, the bonus is to remain ⅔ of revenue per worker, now equal to $8.17 (⅔ × $36.76), GM will insist on lowering the base wage by 17¢, from $16 to $15.83.

In all systems there is no escaping the real consequences of a permanent increase in the cost of imported raw materials. Consumers must cut back on using such materials and turn to other commodities. However, a share system delays the inflationary impact and disemploys labor not directly by firing workers, but indirectly, only after relative pay has been lowered so that workers are induced to look elsewhere for jobs (and are never actually without work). Although the lowering of share-contract parameters causes an initial decline in pay, it will automatically float back up to the competitive level as workers leave the firm of their own accord, causing revenues per worker to rise. In this example, when GM lowers the base wage from $16 to $15.83 under the new contract, the immediate effect is to lower a worker's pay by 17¢ below the competitive level of $24. (A more realistic, but ultimately equivalent, scenario is that pay increases at GM do not keep pace with economy-wide productivity advances.) Although at this point GM would prefer its workers to stay, the discrepancy with the competitive wage available elsewhere will cause the eventual emigration of 6.2 percent of its work force to other jobs, until revenues per worker rise by 76¢ to $36.76, at which point a new state of long-run equilibrium has been attained and GM workers are again paid $24 per hour. If the imported materials are used by every firm in the economy, not just GM, a price rise must cause a general decline in the standard of living and in real wages. But, again, the inflationary impact is delayed under a share system and there is no unemployment.

Consider next what would happen if a share firm were subject to a cost-push shock and forced for some reason to raise its pay above the competitive level by setting "too high" values of the parameters of the share contract. If a wage firm were forced to pay a higher wage, it would decrease employment and raise the price of its output. In contrast, under a share contract the profit-maximizing firm would offset any pay increase above the competitive rate by hiring more labor, increasing output, and lowering price. Of course profits are smaller if pay parameters are artificially raised above competitive values; and the share firm will end up with labor's marginal value less than its average cost (but above its marginal cost). In both systems the economy-wide response to such artificial cost-push pay raises, should they stick, is to misallocate resources by discouraging overall investment and by encouraging firms to buy labor-substituting rather than labor-complementing machines. But the share firm does not pass through an artificial pay increase into fewer jobs or higher prices, whereas a wage firm does. Even should labor succeed in getting a larger than competitive portion of the income pie, any damage to resource allocation under a share system is indirect and confined to long-run inefficiencies, by causing the increase in present labor income to come at the expense of future income, but without spilling over into unemployment or inflation.

To use my favorite scenario once again, suppose the prevailing competitive remuneration (including benefits) for the skill level of a GM auto worker is $24 per hour. The firm is in profit-maximizing equilibrium; the marginal revenue produced by an extra worker is also $24 per hour. The average revenue per worker hour is $36. If GM is operating under a wage system and the UAW succeeds in pushing wages up to $25 per hour, GM will respond by laying off workers, contracting output, and raising the price of its automobiles. Of course the tenured high-seniority workers are better off because they are making a dollar an hour more, which maybe helps to explain why such things occur.

But now look at what happens in a share system. Suppose GM was in equilibrium competitively paying a base wage of $16 plus a bonus share of ⅔ of revenue per worker. At that point GM desires to hire more labor but can't find any more workers. Now say the UAW pushes the base wage up by $1 per hour, from $16 to $17. (The analysis is essentially the same if the UAW artificially forces up the share parameter, say from ⅔ to ¼ of revenue per worker, which also yields an initial increase in pay of $1 per hour.) The immediate effect is to raise each GM worker's pay to $25 per hour. That will naturally make GM worse off. But given the pay contract it is now stuck with, GM can still increase profits by hiring more labor. Only now it is in a position to do something about attracting additional workers, maybe not immediately but eventually, because it is currently paying one dollar above the going market rate.

So GM will hire more workers, increasing production, lowering the price of its automobiles, decreasing the reve-

117
Life in a Share Economy *profit*

nue per worker, and causing the share element to decline by $1 per hour or until pay comes back down to the competitive level of $24 per hour and GM can draw no additional labor. The adjustment process may take some time, but its end result is clear. Afterwards GM is making less profits than under the competitive arrangement, but making more profits than if it had not responded to the artificial pay increase by hiring additional labor and selling more automobiles at a lower price. And labor ends up being paid the going rate. These basic conclusions must hold even when several unions are trying to push up pay parameters above the levels employers would wish to select. So long as there is decentralized contract bargaining, it is probably harder for labor to claim a higher pay level under a share system than under a wage system.

It is especially difficult, then, for cost-push inflation to get even a toehold in a share firm. Any raising of labor's pay above the going level is a temporary effect that the firm will automatically offset, over time, by hiring new workers attracted to its higher compensation and by flooding its product market with low-priced output. The share system thus has a kind of self-cleansing tendency that spontaneously discourages local outbreaks of cost-plus infestations. It is impossible for the workers of a share firm to always get paid above the prevailing level for decades on end. A share system promises full employment for all at the competitive rate. But unlike a wage system, no privileged subgroup of workers can aspire to succeed, at the expense of disemploying fellow workers and raising prices, in permanently extorting an overambitious level of pay artificially raised above what others are getting for comparable work. (It is this aspiration that provides a major part of the initial impetus to wage-push inflation.)

In a share firm, furthermore, there is no obscuring the fact that one claimant's share of the income pie can only be increased at the direct expense of another's. By dispelling the illusion that inconsistent claims can be fobbed off on a third party, a share system should help to foster an environment of greater natural resistance to the unwarranted demands that initiate a wage-price spiral. All things considered, the effect must be to derail the cost-push locomotive before it can gather inflationary momentum. It would thus appear that the share system, with its excess demand for workers, introduces an all-round strengthening of competitive forces into the labor market and a considerably more robust egalitarian tendency for pay per unit skill level to be equalized throughout the economy.

Broadly speaking, we are accustomed to thinking of economic recovery as a time of upward pressure on prices because, in a wage system, expansion to get out of a recession is typically stimulated by increased aggregate demand. Any tendency of a wage system toward buoyant employment depends on a somewhat extraneous pull from increased spending — typically private investment or public expenditures. But in a share system the absorption of unemployed labor originates primarily on the supply side, which puts downward pressure on output prices. Share firms in equilibrium want to reduce their prices further by producing more output and moving down their demand curve, but are held back because they cannot find any unemployed labor to hire.

We have already seen that the predominance of product markets where price exceeds marginal cost has important economic and sociological consequences. When sellers set

prices so that supply exceeds demand, they are uncon-
sciously creating an environment where they must chase
after and win over their prospective buyers. Capitalism
gratifies its consumers greatly; they are wooed and pam-
pered, their needs and whims attended to and even anticipated.

But capitalism does not treat its workers with anything
remotely resembling the same level of devotion. Too many
are left unemployed through no fault of their own. Many
jobs are unpleasant and often, it seems, unnecessarily so.
Working conditions are frequently demeaning, and the
workplace is commonly a crowded, noisy, dirty, or otherwise distasteful environment. Permeating the entire system is the grimly accepted fact that, when all is said and
done, the employer really doesn't care about the employee.

One party "cares" for another in a commercial setting
only when there is something to be gained from it. The firm
cares about a customer because an extra sale is worth more
than it costs. The firm paying a wage does not care about a
worker because the extra value created by that worker just
balances the extra cost. In such cases the firm is essentially
indifferent to whether the worker stays or goes. Naturally
the worker feels alienated. But when a firm pays labor with
a share of its own revenues or profits, it cares about the
worker because the extra value being created exceeds the
extra cost. The share firm wants its workers to stay and
even to work more hours; it cares about whether they leave
or not.

The forces of self-interest will lead the firms of a share
economy to create in the labor market a rich panoply of
nonprice competition for workers, analogous to what we
are accustomed to observing in output markets. Share firms
will advertise for and seek out workers because more help

is always wanted even while the economy is at full employment. Innovative recruitment and training procedures will spring up. Personnel officers, instead of sitting at their desks passively accepting applications from job seekers begging for work under a wage system, now will actively compete in searching out qualified candidates whom they may have the privilege of interviewing and possibly hiring. (Of course the profits so made by taking on extra workers are transitory and fleeting, but they are nonetheless real for that.) Thus a share economy means no involuntarily unemployed workers looking for jobs and no discouraged workers who have given up and dropped out of the labor market.

The benefits of an excess demand for labor without inflation are considerable.[3] There are the extra goods and services produced by a fully utilized economy. There is the inevitable reduction of poverty and inequality that goes along with full employment as people earn their way to higher incomes. There is the security of workers knowing their present job can be kept because a share firm de facto offers lifetime employment; and even if a job should be lost or a worker wishes to transfer, another job can be found relatively easily in a share economy. There are the future benefits from growth and technological progress when capital formation is spurred on by steady brisk demand at full capacity and is relatively unhampered by fears of automation. There are the gains, international as well as national, of free trade and open markets when a country does not have to worry about protectionist measures to prop up declining industries and save jobs at home. (The prospect of strong export-led growth in an enduring world economic boom is worth considerably more to the underdeveloped nations than the current value of all foreign aid programs.)

There is the promise, when the threat of stagflation is removed, of being better able to concentrate on the real economic choices and problems that confront a society — and there is the hope of being in a better position to do something constructive about them when the public-sector budget is less tightly squeezed.

There is another, more subtle benefit of permanent excess demand for labor. It gives dignity to the working man and woman, the sense of being significant, useful members of society. When workers are scarce and employers want them, working conditions will be improved. This is an inevitable consequence of the nonprice competition that must take place in the labor markets of a share economy whose workers, as well as consumers, are free to choose. Firms competing for workers will apply to the problem of making work more attractive some of the considerable ingenuity they have demonstrated in luring customers to their products. When it is in the economic interest of an employer to please his workers, he will very quickly discover what makes them happy and endeavor to bring it about. The welfare of a firm's workers will vie with the quality of its products as an important goal. The worker's greatest protection is his power to get a job elsewhere — that threat can do more to improve working conditions than legislation, standards, or collective militancy.

When firms are hungry for labor, there is little place for nonfunctional discrimination. Prejudices unrelated to actual productivity may be deeply rooted, but so is the profit motive. Any difference in the treatment, pay, or hiring of workers which is not related to job performance can persist as a systematic tendency only when firms do not actually need the workers they have the luxury of being prejudiced against. Rosy the Riveter had no trouble finding a well-paying job during the severe labor shortage of World War II, but she was thrown out of work after the labor market returned to more "normal" conditions. In the generally tight labor market prevailing during the period from the beginning of World War II to the end of the Korean War (when nonwhite unemployment averaged under 5 percent), millions of black workers advanced themselves economically by moving out of the rural south to attain jobs in the industrial north. I suspect that, over time, permanent excess demand for labor can do more to reduce or eliminate nonfunctional discrimination in the job market than all of the regulations, quotas, and affirmative-action programs currently in existence.

Are these utopian dreams? I think not. Modern industrial capitalism with its large-scale enterprises and its tremendous potential for economic growth is a relatively recent episode in history, bursting upon the world scene a mere century or two ago. It is very much in a state of change and adaptation now, little resembling a fully evolved mechanism. As a system, capitalism has half-blindly stumbled onto certain performance modes, with some current ones being permanent (or as permanent as any social institution can be), others of questionable value, and a few downright self-defeating. Alienation of workers, the power of capital over labor, and the reserve army of the unemployed are specific consequences of the wage mode, not universal characteristics of the capitalist system. Sooner or later it will be realized that a share version of capitalism greatly outperforms a wage version, and something will be done about it. In economics as elsewhere, the tyranny of the status quo has enormous inertia. But it cannot hold out indefinitely against reasonable change when the economy is so visibly malfunctioning as ours is under stagflation.

9
Vaccinating Capitalism
Against Stagflation

I F A SHARE SYSTEM DOES represent a far better way of operating a market economy than a wage system, why don't we see more examples of share economies? After all, even the Japanese have taken only a modest (although significant) step in this direction. The rest of the advanced capitalist countries are predominantly wage economies.

The answer to the question involves what economists variously call an "externality," a "public good," or a "market failure."[1] A typical example of this sort of phenomenon is automobile pollution. Today every new car must comply with federally mandated emission standards. The required antipollution equipment costs several hundreds of dollars per automobile to manufacture and install. Given a free choice, most consumers would decide not to buy the anti-pollution devices, thereby saving up to $300 on the price of a new car. After all, only a negligible fraction of the pollution emitted by my car hurts me — most of it is dissipated into the air and bothers other people. Yet when every car buyer reasons this way, we all end up with an unpleasantly polluted environment that costs us much more than the equivalent of a one-time $300 per automobile fee in terms of health and comfort.

The essence of the externality problem pertaining to labor compensation is that, in choosing a particular contract form, the firm and its workers only calculate the effect on themselves. They take no account of the possible effects on the rest of the economy. The firm and its workers do not have an incentive to consider the macroeconomic implications of the contract form they are selecting. Yet, as we have seen, the macroeconomic implications of choosing between a wage system and share system are considerable.

When a firm and its workers select a share form of labor contract, they are contributing to an atmosphere of full employment and brisk aggregate demand without inflation. But these macroeconomic advantages do not properly accrue to those who make the decision. Like clean air, the benefits are spread throughout the community. The wage firm and its workers do not have the correct incentives to cease polluting the macroeconomic environment by converting to a share contract.

Viewed this way, involuntary unemployment is far and away the costliest market failure of capitalism. If we could get rid of this externality, there would be enough surplus generated to pay easily for correcting air pollution and all of the other, more standard examples of market failure. There is an enormous social payoff to an effective and polit-

ically acceptable mechanism for ridding the macroeconomic environment of unemployment.

The share economy owes its superior properties to a kind
of benign balance of forces that takes place when there is a
critical mass of share firms. If any one share firm could
succeed in finding a source of unemployed labor to hire,
that would temporarily lower the compensation of its employees in the short run. But when there are many share
firms, there will be no significant pockets of involuntarily
unemployed workers waiting around to be hired (since they
will already have been absorbed by the other share firms),
and this pay-reducing mechanism will never be fully acti-
vated. It is the potential lowering of pay that would occur in
the short run if more workers could be hired by a share firm
that, paradoxically, actually keeps everyone employed at
good pay in a share system.

That part changes when the share firms constitute a
small minority. Should one firm alone in a prevailing wage
system go over to a share contract, it will be guaranteeing
full employment to its own workers and serving as the employer of last resort for the others. If the decline in demand
for GM products previously analyzed now applies to other
firms as well, GM *alone* on a share contract might be
tempted to hire every unemployed worker in the state of
Michigan. When contractionary shocks are correlated
across the economy, in bad times the single share firm will
be absorbing unemployed labor shed by all the depressed
wage firms (this is the externality), thereby lowering the
pay of its original workers, possibly well below the competitive full-employment level. If all or at least many wage
firms go to a share system, every worker and the economy
as a whole benefit from the resulting tight labor market,
full employment, and consequent high level of demand

spending. But it is not at all clear that the already employed workers of an existing firm in a wage system will benefit if that firm alone converts to a share contract. (It depends in a complicated way on many factors, including the form of demand uncertainty and the particular features of the contract.)

Furthermore, even if all major firms are on share contracts, there is always a temptation for the individual share firm to become a free rider. The full-employment pay level represents the effective terms of trade on which any company in a share economy can obtain labor. If one share firm converts to a wage contract paying the prevailing level of compensation, it loses nothing and gains the added short-run flexibility of being able to lay off workers freely when its business is bad and take on more of them when business is good. Nor do the workers care that much because there are always jobs available in a share system. But if all firms in the share economy try to become free riders by changing to a wage contract, that will facilitate the mass layoffs and spending contractions that feed back into lowering every firm's profits.

A share system thus has some tendency to be an unstable social institution under individualistic decision making. What is sensible private behavior need not be in the public interest. The essence of the public-good aspect of the problem is that, in choosing between contract forms, the firm and its workers do not take into account the employment effects on the labor market as a whole and the consequent spending implications for aggregate demand. The macroeconomic externality of a tight labor market is helped by a share contract and hurt by a wage contract, but the difference is uncompensated. In such situations there can be no presumption that the economy is optimally organized. Even

Vaccinating Capitalism Against Stagflation

democratic majority rule would not necessarily attain a social optimum because the principle of one-man-one-vote cannot register the *intensity* of disutility suffered by those without work. In effect, the unemployed or about-to-be-unemployed members of a wage economy are disenfranchised outsiders who bear the costs of stopping inflation and of providing a stable wage for the majority of insiders enjoying steady employment and rarely facing layoffs.

Wherever there is a significant externality, there is a prima facie case for collective action to encourage everyone to do what is in their joint interest but not in their selfish private interest. Abraham Lincoln said it nicely: "The legitimate object of government is to do for a community of people, whatever they need to have done, but can not do *at all*, or can not *so well do*, for themselves — in their separate and individual capacities."

If the externality is important enough, the government, acting in the national interest, must change the private reward structure so that each person is induced to do what will actually make him or her better off when everyone else is also induced to do it. Returning to the analogy of the baseball stadium crowd spontaneously standing up in anticipation of a big play, the best way to keep everybody seated is to levy a fine on anyone caught standing or to pay a reward to anyone remaining seated. (You can see how idealized this example is becoming.) If the fine is stiff enough, no one actually pays it because all remain seated. And then everybody has a better view from a more comfortable position than when they were all standing.

I would like to sketch out what I think are reasonable policy measures for encouraging an economy to convert from a wage system to a share system. But there is nothing sacrosanct about the particular approach or the details.

Alternatives are possible, and some may be superior. The issue at this point is one of political reality, not economic theory. Should the basic rationale of the share approach become familiar and acceptable, then over time the experience and collaboration of practical minds will eventually elaborate the most appropriate implementation strategy. The key phrase here is: where there is a will there is a way. If we have the courage as a society to look beyond defeatism, inertia, nitpicking, and short-sighted self-interest, we can put in place any one of several perfectly operational incentive structures that will make us all better off.

The number of share firms needed to make a share system work is not very large. Many people are not aware just how concentrated American industry is. The 500 largest corporations hire more than a third of the nation's privately employed non-agricultural labor force, including over three fourths of all workers employed in manufacturing.

To change from a wage economy to a share economy, we need a high-priority, vigorous national program stressing awareness, education, and information to infuse a sense of social responsibility into the collective-bargaining process. Without strong visible leadership from important people, the indispensable climate of public opinion required to sustain such an effort cannot be generated. Unions, corporations, and ordinary citizens need to understand what would be accomplished by going over to a share system—and what is at stake. Counseling services should be made readily available, staffed by knowledgeable, motivated, well-trained (and well-paid) experts, to explain about various gain-sharing plans and to offer specific help on implementation. There should also be an extensive and useful library of publications. A general atmosphere ought to be created where share contracts are sympathetically viewed by the community at large as being socially beneficial. Collective-bargaining agreements with a large share component should be publicly praised because they are helping all of society, whereas wage contracts should be frowned upon because they serve narrow interests and hurt society. We should not hesitate to exploit such propagandistic means to help create "the greatest good for the greatest number." But above and beyond any jawboning or raising of social consciousness, we must not shirk from using strong tax incentives. We must make it in people's self-interest that each should give a little so that all may gain a lot.

There are two broad classes of income: earned income (the return to labor that constitutes about 80 percent of national income) and unearned income (the return to property constituting the other 20 percent). In United States tax law there are several privileged subcategories of unearned income: long-term capital gains (60 percent tax-free), interest on municipal bonds (100 percent tax-free), corporate dividends ($100 tax exclusion), gas and oil depletion allowances (16 percent of production income tax-free), investment tax credits, extraordinarily accelerated writeoff schedules for depreciating business property (economic life less than one third of actual life), bizarre psuedo-leasing arrangements for capital equipment, and so on and on. What is striking is how extremely imaginative Congress has been in dreaming up lucrative subcategories of unearned income to save taxes for certain privileged classes of people, but how relatively shy they have been to repeat that same sort of special treatment for earned income.

Why should it be primarily the rich who have special shelters where they can direct their money to save taxes, with the blessing of the government? Why should not working people also get a tax break on a legislated subcategory of earned income, if that is clearly in the national interest?

I propose that the earned income of employees of private corporations whose shares are publicly traded be divided into two subcategories — wage income and share income — which are taxed differently. Wage income, that component paid at a fixed dollar rate (or linked to the consumer price index), is taxed as usual at ordinary rates. But a tax break is given to share income; say one half of share income is tax-exempt up to some reasonable ceiling, taxes being paid only on the remaining half.

Although no important issue of principle is involved, on practical grounds it might be a good idea initially to limit the tax-exempt treatment of share income to employees of private corporations whose shares are publicly owned. One reason is that such firms are already required to regularly publish information about sales and earnings by fairly well-established accounting criteria, which they are unlikely to be tempted to manipulate. Another reason is that on grounds of fairness it makes sense to distinguish the sharelike income of self-employed persons and small partnerships, which is "naturally" tied to the value of what the individual produces, from the share income of workers belonging to a division-of-labor team in a large firm, which is dependent upon forces utterly outside the individual's control. Besides, self-employed workers along with employees of government and nonprofit institutions are not afflicted by unemployment nearly so badly as others. From a pragmatic standpoint, the reform is aimed at eliminating unemployment by turning private firms into selective employers of last resort whose current employees may conceivably bear some burden. For this potential burden of lower pay, which does not actually materialize to any significant degree in a share economy (but whose presence does eliminate unemployment), share workers are entitled to a tax reward.

The 50 percent tax exemption (up to a reasonable income ceiling) represents a compromise figure, and there is nothing sacred about that particular fraction. It should be high enough to induce a significant number of companies and their employees to try some share arrangement for at least one contract period — independent of the state of the economy or what other companies are doing. Yet such a fraction, applied to a limited subcategory of income, should be easily made up by the much higher tax receipts and much lower welfare expenditures of a permanently booming full-employment economy. Preliminary calculations performed to estimate the orders of magnitude involved indicate that the particular tax-reduction formula proposed here would break even and pay for itself as a tax reform if it reduced the national unemployment rate by an average of just one percentage point.[2] (These strong conclusions come from facts such as: jobless people pay almost no taxes, half of them receive unemployment compensation, their families are more likely to be on welfare. These and a multitude of other recessionary drains on the government budget are extremely substantial, amounting to hundreds of billions of dollars a year during severe contractions. Every extra percentage point of unemployment translates into about $25 billion of increased federal budget deficits and about $80 billion of permanently lost GNP per year.) Of course different tax formulas or parameters are possible, and may well be desirable, but the main idea should be clear. Nor must we think of any particular tax formulation as immutable over time. Actually, an experimental or sequential approach might be exactly what is called for in the circumstances.

This is supply-side economics par excellence. But I would hope that the reader can see that behind it stands a coherent theory and a genuine logic based upon the reemployment of idle resources. The same cannot be said for the cocktail-napkin version proposed by Arthur Laffer and his colleagues.[3]

The operational test of share income is whether or not it is significantly dependent on the corporation's state of "profitability per employee." To qualify as share income, compensation must be explicitly linked by written formula to such relevant indices of the firm as near-current profits per worker or sales per worker. The formula itself must be reasonably stable over some time period, say no less than one half year's duration. And one other criterion is required: there must be no collusive or other restraining of the share firm from actively recruiting as many workers as would be profitable to hire under the formula. (Explicit restraint in the form of a closed shop is already forbidden under existing labor legislation.)

This last requirement may be important. The mere fact that we live primarily in a wage system is indirect evidence that powerful forces of self-interest are out there to subvert basic reforms in the way labor is paid. My approach takes as given the age-old hallmark of capitalism: private ownership of the means of production, where the decisions on output, employment, and pricing are essentially made by capitalists. I personally think that capitalism is a pretty sturdy system; so there is little danger of upsetting its bedrock, even if we should want to, by the kinds of reforms being discussed here. After all, under both wage and share contracts the welfare of a union's members depends critically on the firm's employment decisions, and in both cases a union would like to assume more control. I can see no compelling reason why a capitalist firm should be more prone to allow increased worker participation in company decision making under one contract form than under another. Nevertheless if, for any reason, the move toward a share economy leads to increased collusion on restricting new hiring, the share principle and all that it implies will be jeopardized.[4] Just to make sure, therefore, that the share system functions as it is intended to, for the workers of a union shop to be eligible to receive the considerable tax benefits from being paid in share income, both union and management must forswear any restrictive hiring practices. No union is compelled to petition for the special tax status of a share plan. But when it chooses to participate, a union cannot enjoy the tax benefits without reaffirming an already existing legal commitment to open its ranks to as many qualified members and apprentices as the company wishes to hire under the agreed-upon share contract. This is a logical requirement for the government to insist on, since the entire raison d'être of the differential tax treatment is to encourage increased employment.

Although union members represent a minority of the United States labor force (some 20 percent), they are more widespread among industrial workers (about 40 percent). Because the business cycle is played out to a large degree in the industrial sector, it is very important that any program of converting to an economy of share firms extend to unionized firms as well. Some union workers might oppose the adoption of a share plan. High-seniority workers, who possess a disproportionate influence in a union, have relatively less to gain from a share plan because their employment is already fairly stable. And with a higher than competitive wage, union members might conceivably have more to lose from conversion to a share contract because expansion of employment by their firm will erode the earning premium their union position allows. (Studies suggest that the average wage of union workers, corrected for differences in the productivity and selectivity of workers induced by unionization itself, is very roughly about 10 percent higher relative to the average wage of all workers than it would have been in the absence of unionism.[5])

If the incentives are strong enough, however, a unionized firm will not only be enticed to join the share economy, but in a sense will be driven to enroll. It will be compelled because, if many other firms adopt share plans and if the advantages in the form of tax savings are significant enough (larger than the union premium), a union will be unable to compete for members without following course. And, as argued above, the potential tax benefits could be made extremely attractive without doing fiscal harm to the federal budget, since the increases in government revenues and decreases in outlays obtained from maintaining perpetual full employment are so enormous. Actually the potential tax advantage to adopting a share form of compensation would perhaps be even greater for a unionized firm and its workers than for a nonunionized firm. For a variety of reasons, union workers earn more income and are in a higher tax bracket than other workers. Therefore, making a fraction of share income tax-free has greater tax-saving potential for the typical union worker than for the typical nonunion worker.

The role of the government could be as follows. A Share Plan Agency (SPA) is set up as a branch of the Internal Revenue Service. It establishes broad outlines for what

Vaccinating Capitalism Against Stagflation

constitutes a bona-fide share contract, including the criteria previously discussed, and accredits the proposed share plans of eligible publicly held private corporations that wish to take advantage of the new tax law on behalf of their employees.

This is not a coercive reform, nor is it difficult to administer. Some form of profit sharing already exists in over 15 percent of our largest companies. A share economy is not imposed by government, but rather it is created by the participants with the help of government. Such a reform represents a relatively minor adjustment of the private enterprise system that preserves the time-proven advantages of decentralized decision making while allowing the market to improve its performance tremendously. No essential aspect of the existing capitalist order is threatened, nor are traditional roles challenged. The corporations, the unions, and anyone else can do whatever they please within the law. (The government should make it clear at all times where society's interests lie and should not shirk from praise or criticism of a contract *form* in appropriate cases — but that is all.) No one dictates to firms or unions how to set share parameters, whether plans should be voluntary for individual employees or mandatory for all employees, whether or not the various subdivisions of a conglomerate should be treated as autonomous accounting entities, whether reasonable smoothing formulas should be used to adjust seasonal indexes, or what fraction of pay should be wage income and what fraction share income. All that is up to the invisible hand of competition and the visible hand of collective bargaining. There would be no tampering with the National Labor Relations Board or with the basic rights of workers to union representation and collective bargaining to determine pay parameters, working conditions, grievance procedures, and the like, as envisioned in the National Labor Relations Act. The proposed reform does not reward open shops, encourage right-to-work laws, or anything of that sort. The only concrete thing the government does is to allow that half of sensibly defined share income will be tax-free up to some reasonable limit for the eligible employees of publicly held private corporations having a valid SPA-accredited plan. Here is an example of what a typical plan might look like.

GM and the UAW acquiesce in the following three-year contract and then go before the SPA to receive accreditation. A certain agreed-upon fraction of the previous quarter's sales revenues is to be set aside in a special account as a "sharing fund" to be prorated into thirteen equal weekly payments to labor during any current quarter. Each job category is then remunerated by an agreed-upon base wage or core pay and a number of fund shares proportional to the fixed wage. The actual share income received by a worker in a given week is the number of his or her fund shares times the size of the weekly fund payout divided by the total number of shares currently outstanding. The worker's total taxable income, on which current withholding is based, is 100 percent of wage income plus 50 percent of share income. A computer automates the calculation and printing of paychecks, furnishing all relevant information on an accompanying statement that explains why the share income came out to be whatever it is each week. After three years, a new contract is signed along similar lines, but with possibly different parameter values depending upon the company, the union, and the present state of economic conditions.

The two most immediate candidates for inclusion in share plans are revenues per worker and profits per worker, gross or net, calculated by any reasonably consistent definition. (There could be other possibilities — for example, value added per worker — since a fairly wide class of share indexes will have the desired stagflation-fighting properties.) Probably "revenues" is inherently a more precise concept than "profits" and might be better to use for that reason. On the other hand, profits tend to be more stable over time and are a truer measure of the firm's economic condition. (If profits are used, the worker should be offered "limited liability" so that the share component of labor income never goes below zero.) Of course both sales and earnings must already be reported to the Securities and Exchange Commission on a quarterly basis, under fairly well-established accounting procedures, so there is not much room for manipulation here (it is also illegal). A more widespread use of share contracts might lead to greater discussion of accounting conventions and to increased demands by employees that a firm open its books to them. But such developments are perhaps not altogether to be deplored.

There are many other details to be worked out, but the reader would be bored with them — and anyway it is the basic idea that counts. The key thing to note is that this sort of scheme is eminently operational and implementable; it is no more "impractical," "ill-defined," "distributionally undesirable," or "incentive-distorting" than the majority of existing IRS and SEC regulations — or is that damning by faint praise? It is a routine exercise for any economics student to point out the distributional inequities, microeconomic distortions, and allocational inefficiencies inherent in such a tax program. But in our second- or third-best economy (and even in hypothetical versions improved by basic tax reforms), it is not at all clear whether these additional misallocations help or hurt overall efficiency. Besides, the microeconomic distortions are of negligible consequence compared to the macroeconomic costs of underemployed labor and capital.

To the working class, a share system promises permanent full employment at competitive remuneration, no inflation, and an improvement in working conditions and employer attitudes. It asks of the workers that they receive a substantial part of their pay as a negotiated share of company profits or revenues (per employee). For bearing this risk, which is entirely voluntary even though it is in the national interest, they will be well rewarded by significantly lower tax rates. (Incidentally, the argument for using the tax system to encourage socially desirable forms of risk bearing has been used, evidently successfully, to justify the extraordinary preferential tax treatment accorded long-term capital gains.)

It would be a mistake to extrapolate the demand variability now observed in the firms of a wage economy to a share economy. Such cyclical industries as machine tools, metals, building materials, construction, and the like, would not fluctuate nearly so much, since the share economy is permanently operating near full capacity. Every firm of a share system would exhibit significantly greater demand stability than we are now accustomed to because a budding recession cannot feed upon itself in a fully employed economy. Studies show that economy-wide and industry-wide factors currently account for approximately half the sales or earnings variability of the average firm.[6] The advantages to the business and investment communities of a climate of greatly reduced economic fluctuations should prove substantial. An enlarged steady volume of private investment is a likely response to the more stable profit expectations of an economy whose existing plant and equipment are always fully utilized. Government budgets will naturally be less in deficit and far more smoothly balanced over a significantly dampened business cycle. And a share contract itself will look more attractive to a worker in the less variable environment of a share economy.

People and institutions will adapt to a share structure. One can hedge against lower corporate earnings, to a significant extent, by selling company stock short. (And if a worker in a big corporation doesn't know how to do this himself, some enterprising insurance company is sure to come around with a neatly packaged policy offering to insure share fluctuations for a premium.) Industries with inherently greater variability may offset more volatile share income by paying higher than average compensation, or they may just choose to offer wages alone and forgo the tax advantages of the share contract. (For instance, it may be unreasonable to suppose that a new firm would be able to attract labor by offering to pay share income.) A worker with a particular degree of risk aversion will be able to find a niche easily enough in a share economy because there is permanent excess demand for labor as a whole.

It is worth emphasizing that a wage system does not offer labor as a whole a less risky compensation than a share system. It is *not* true that in a share economy workers are bearing the risk, while in a wage economy firms are bearing the risk. The theory that firms on wage contracts are implicitly insuring their homogeneous pool of risk-averse workers against income variability is a fallacious generalization of the tenured worker's experience in a partial-equilibrium setting.[7] Anyone who seriously entertains such a notion might soberly contemplate explaining the insurance benefits to a nontenured worker who has just been laid off. The firm's total labor force typically receives more real income during a recession from a share system than from a wage system. The relevant issue is not whether the firm's pool of workers should put all their eggs in one basket—they each did that already when they went to work for a single company—but rather which type of basket is more crush-resistant for whom.

No compensation system can be risk-free for everybody. If there are risks inherent in the conduct of economic affairs, some agents must bear them. But the wage system, contrary to the "market knows best" doctrine, actually represents a bad risk-sharing arrangement for society as a whole, because of the strong negative macroeconomic effects on aggregate employment and demand. A share system is no more risky overall than a wage system, and considerably less so in the relevant real economic variables. It is just that the form and impact of the uncertainty are different. A share economy stabilizes the aggregate output (and consumption) of goods and services at the full-employment level, while permitting nominal incomes to adjust. A wage economy stabilizes the nominal pay of a high-seniority worker, but only at the expense of loading unemployment on low-seniority workers, and inflation on everybody— hence greatly destabilizing the real income of the working class as a whole.

Workers who have chosen a share plan may have to learn to save more on a regular basis. That is perhaps not altogether a bad thing. Personal savings rates in the United States, for example, are much too low by most reasonable calculations. In Japan, the bonus system is probably a contributing factor to the impressively high rate of savings among the working class.[8] An unfortunate legacy of the Keynesian tradition is the apprehension that too much saving makes a wage economy more prone toward unemployment and stagnation. Keynes and other underconsumptionists laid great stress on the paradox of thrift, the idea that the private virtue of high saving may actually be a public vice because it depresses aggregate demand. As for the loss of capital accumulation from low investment of existing output, that takes its toll only in the long run — and of course it makes much more sense to concentrate on the immediate problem of unemployment because, as Keynes once colorfully put it, "in the long run we are all dead." The automatic full employment of the share economy frees the system from this sort of stagnationist pessimism about high savings rates and creates the kind of environment where capital accumulation can develop naturally at a more rapid pace.

10
Is It Practical?

I N THIS BOOK I HAVE ARGUED
that the average worker, as well as the economy as a whole,
would be better off under a share system. There are many
reasons why it is a good idea for a significant part of the
pay of employees to be linked directly to some index of their
firm's well-being. But, as with boiled eggs, it is useful to
consider three basic kinds.

A "soft-boiled" reason is that gain sharing (contingent
compensation schemes) can boost employee morale, increase worker participation, improve labor-management
relations, foster a sense of partnership, raise productivity,
and so forth. This aspect has been duly noted by industrial-
relations experts for years, even to the point of being actively promoted by some as a money-making proposition

for employers. The argument undoubtedly contains an important germ of truth, although it is difficult to believe that incentive effects alone could make a significant difference at the level of macroeconomic performance. Note that the benefits in the soft-boiled version are strictly private, so there is no really legitimate case for social policy.

A "medium-boiled" argument holds that gain sharing is good simply because greater aggregate wage flexibility is desirable per se. When wages are automatically made more sensitive to economic conditions, so goes the argument, that cannot help improving macroeconomic performance. Once the government has caused a policy-induced recession, the economy's natural self-correcting forces (based on reductions in the rate of wage-push inflation) are eventually supposed to rectify the situation. If the cause of the inflationary persistence is that wage-setting behavior does not heed the signal of tight money or austere fiscal policy (or it simply cannot during the period between wage bargains), then tying pay to any index correlated with the health of the national economy (including industry-specific or firm-specific indexes) should assist by making wages more directly and more quickly responsive to aggregate policy.[1]

There is no doubt a great deal of truth to the medium-boiled argument. This kind of business-cycle indexing would moderate inflation by improving the efficiency of a wage economy's self-correcting mechanism without building in an inexorably rising floor under labor costs. And there may be a genuine case here for government intervention because of the externality aspect. (But on the employment side, beware the fallacy of composition—more flexible aggregate wages per se may not be terribly useful in fighting unemployment.) All things considered, it seems plausible to suppose that less rigid wages will help to stabilize employment and to even out government budget imbalances and corporate profits over the business cycle.

While the soft-boiled and medium-boiled versions of the case for gain sharing have genuine merit, this book stakes out what I like to think of as a "hard-boiled" rationale. When the pay of employees is linked to their particular firm's performance, the very nature of the economy's modus operandi changes in a fundamental way. (Note that, unlike the medium-boiled case, this effect cannot be obtained by indexing wages to national or even industry-wide economic conditions.) A share system has the hard-boiled property of excess demand for labor, which turns it into a tenacious natural enemy of stagnation and inflation. The share economy possesses a built-in, three-pronged assault on unemployment, stagnant output, and the tendency of prices to rise. That is a hard combination to beat.

But is the concept of fundamental wage reform practical? Can it be done? Can a wage economy be turned into a share economy?

On the practicality of fundamental change, Benjamin Disraeli once remarked that a practical man appears to be one who "practices the errors of his forefathers." Although speaking half in jest, the great leader of popular conservatism was trying to make a serious point about a problem he frequently confronted. Any fundamental reform, even reasonable change that is needed to *conserve* the existing order, will routinely be labeled "impractical." But what the reflex naysayers are really reacting to is primarily the fact that it just hasn't been done before.

The political feasibility of basic economic reform depends not only upon its intrinsic merits but also upon the urgency of the underlying problem and the extent to which it is realized that the traditional approach has failed. We are already well on our way to recognizing that stagflation — the premier economic malady of our time — cannot be cured by traditional monetary-fiscal policies but will require new remedies, of necessity unconventional and unproven. Were we to move in the direction of a share economy, I am sure that future generations would wonder how it could ever have been otherwise.

Criticisms can be leveled against any proposal to change fundamentally the nature of labor remuneration in the major firms of an economy. I am not, I think, unaware of their strong points and have attempted to deal with several of them in passing. Yet when all is said and done, I have not so far encountered a convincing argument against the share-economy principle. The case for at least experimenting with this approach seems compelling. No one is saying that the share concept is a perfect solution for dealing with stagflation. But what are the alternatives?

For centuries, slavish adherence to the gold standard hindered real economic progress. To oppose using gold as the ultimate unit of value was in times past to go against all prevailing orthodoxy. Painfully, after much damage, we came to shed our addiction to the barbarous metal and to stop crucifying mankind upon a cross of gold. We now know that a nation is asking for trouble if it binds its currency to an antique monetary system. The gold standard has passed into history, where it belongs.

But we have not yet shed our addiction to an outmoded system of paying labor. The sacred cross we continue to bear is the "wage standard." To that cross we have nailed untold generations of economic prosperity—many tens, even hundreds, of trillions of present dollars' worth of lost goods and services—sacrificed for the dubious merit of allowing a nation's labor to serve as a hired factor at the pleasure of its capital, rather than as an economy-wide partner in production.

The wage standard is not any kind of universal, inevitable consequence of divine forces, natural laws, or even human nature. It is merely one particular, and rather arbitrary, short-term mechanism for dividing the national product pie among the different groups and classes that contribute to its making. The long-run tendencies of income distribution under capitalism *do* involve deep issues of political economy, perhaps even system-free, tamper-resistant laws. But the selection of a particular disbursement formula to pay claimants is purely the human choice of an institutional arrangement. As human beings guided by the forces of history have made the wage system, so can they, if they wish, unmake it and put in its place something better.

Those who clamor for an "industrial policy" to improve capitalism need look no further than a change in the way workers of large industrial corporations are compensated. Just let labor be paid on a share system—and turn loose the dogs of competition. That simple change will unleash more powerful forces for economic prosperity and social progress than are to be found in the wildest visions of national planners or cultural revolutionaries.

Notes
References
Index

Notes

1. There Is a Better Way

1. The word was coined by Samuelson (1974). The idea that the war against stagflation dominates the current economic agenda is widespread. A forceful statement of the position is contained in Meade (1978, 1982). See also Okun (1977).

2. Three Major Decisions of the Firm

1. The theoretical part of this chapter constitutes the theory of the monopolistically competitive firm. A detailed treatment can be found in any standard economics textbook. See also Chamberlin (1933) and, especially, Lancaster (1979).

2. See Schumpeter (1942).

3. The Coordination Problem of a Market Economy

1. I am trying to describe the equilibrium state of a monopolistically competitive economy — the underlying norm being the "most perfect" competition possible under increasing returns to scale. I regard this as the most appropriate microeconomic foundation for macroeconomic theory. See Weitzman (1982) and the references cited there for more details. See also Kaldor (1972, 1983) on the relationship with perfectly competitive general-equilibrium theory.

2. A good survey of labor market theories is contained in Marshall (1979).

3. For more on this interpretation see Scitovsky (1978).

4. The idea that monopolistic competition can fruitfully be viewed as a system exhibiting excess supply of products does not originate with me. Although the formulation and examples of this chapter are primarily my own invention, I am drawing on the unpublished works and lecture notes of my teachers and colleagues Robert L. Bishop and Evsey D. Domar. See also Bishop (1964), Sraffa (1926), Knight (1923), Young (1928), Kornai (1980).

5. This description of Soviet economic life is my own, but the reader who desires more background might consult Berliner (1976) or Kornai (1983) and the references cited there.

6. See the essays by Hobson, Lenin, and Woolf collected in Wright (1961). See also Luxemburg (1913).

4. The Wage System in a Changing World

1. I am stretching terminology to include under the phrase "rational expectation" any equilibrium-like approach to macroeconomic theory which uses actuarially determined probabilities of various risk-states, and assumes all markets function as well as they can, if not perfectly. A strong form is described in Lucas (1977), Lucas and Sargent (1978), Grossman (1981), and Willes

(1981). Methodologically related weaker forms are typically modified by the inclusion of informational restrictions, transactions costs, or other realistic constraints. This broad category includes, in my view, so-called implicit contract theory. See e.g. Azariadis (1981), Azariadis and Stiglitz (1983), or Hart (1983), and the references cited there. The key distinction between rational expectations and Keynesian approaches to macroeconomic theory, as I see it, hinges on the treatment of long-term expectations. Are they to be viewed primarily as unbiased forecasts endogenously generated within the context of a stochastic equilibrium model having well-defined probability risks? Or are long-term expectations more like autonomously given, essentially unpredictable manifestations of uncertainty-ignorance which can themselves serve as a source of shocks in what is fundamentally a disequilibrium situation? In principle one can look at the matter either way, but it can be argued that the latter way is more relevant for most of the macroeconomic issues of our world.

2. If Keynes were alive today, his first reaction to most contemporary mathematical models of macroeconomics might well be to raise deep objections against what he would view as their basically classical treatment of expectations. For Keynes held that the core of macroeconomics in general, and of the investment decision in particular, involves uncertainty ("the dark forces of time and ignorance") rather than risk (which creates a world no different in essence from classical equilibrium theory). On the distinction between risk and uncertainty and its relevance to macroeconomics, see Keynes (1921, 1936 chap. 12, 1937). See also Knight (1921) and Shackle (1949). For pertinent views on the current state of macroeconomic theory, see Solow (1979, 1980), Tobin (1980, 1983), and the references cited there.

5. Keynes and the Wage Issue

1. A good popular exposition of the Keynesian revolution is contained in Lekachman (1966). My own presentation of Keynes

is naturally skewed toward viewing his ideas in the light of issues raised by this book.

2. Pigou (1933).

3. See the excellent critical discussion in Tobin (1947).

4. Pigou (1937).

5. Meade (1975), p. 88.

6. As just a sample see Nordhaus (1983), Thurow (1983), Bell and Kristol (1981), Hicks (1974, 1983), Tobin (1983).

6. An Uninvited Guest Who Came to Stay

1. See Friedman (1968, 1979 chap. 9).

2. Samuelson (1974), p. 802.

3. Solow (1975), p. 60. This article provides an excellent, readable survey of inflation.

7. Back to Basics

1. See Ackley (1976).

2. See Galenson (1976).

3. Glazer (1976).

4. This is an interpretation of the Japanese experience, but I believe it can be amply supported by the existing literature. See Galenson (1976), OECD (1973), Taira (1970), Nakamura (1983), Odaka (1975), and the many references cited throughout. There is a real need for more primary-source research in this area.

5. For a survey of the classical sharecropping literature, see Cheung (1969). The enclosure movement was essentially a historical change in property rights whereby open-field agriculture — basically a low-rent, common-property share system — gradually became transformed into closed-field agriculture — basically a high-rent, private-property wage system. See Cohen and Weitzman (1975) and the references cited there.

6. Ashley (1903).

7. Tinbergen (1969), p. 18.

8. Trow (1892).

9. Munro (1885).

10. Smart (1894).

11. Carnegie (1900).

12. Lincoln (1909).

13. Lief (1958).

14. See Metzger (1978) and Latta (1979).

15. Berg and Fast (1975) contains a good description of management policies at Lincoln Electric.

16. A mathematical formulation of the model behind this chapter appears in Weitzman (1983).

8. Life in a Share Economy

1. This chapter is based, as is Chapter 7, on the model of Weitzman (1983). See also Weitzman (1982).

2. See Weitzman (1974) for a related analysis.

3. Lerner (1951) contains a good statement of the benefits to high employment. See also Tobin (1965).

9. Vaccinating Capitalism Against Stagflation

1. The general issues are discussed in any standard economics textbook.

2. Suppose, for the sake of argument, that 25 million workers elect to take one half of their pay as share income. The average manufacturing worker now earns about $17,000 per year. If 50 percent of share income is tax-exempt, the annual tax saving per worker comes out to be approximately $1000 (depending on deductions). Under the above assumptions, then, the federal government stands to lose about $25 billion per year in tax revenues. But $25 billion per year is approximately the addition to the budget deficit caused by a one-percentage-point increase in the unem-

ployment rate (*Economic Report of the President,* 1983, p. 26). So if the proposed tax change increases employment by an average of just one percentage point, it pays for itself — and anything above that is translated into a contribution toward a government budget surplus. The interested reader can play with different numbers and see that the conclusions are quite robust.

3. See e.g. Wanniski (1975, 1978).

4. The literature on the worker-managed firm well illustrates this potential threat to new hires. See e.g. Vanek (1970), Meade (1979, 1982), and the references cited there.

5. See Lewis (1963), Reynolds (1982), Hamermesh and Rees (1984).

6. Although the issue I am posing has not been directly addressed, see the somewhat related studies cited in Foster (1978), Ball and Brown (1967). I believe the numbers that emerge from these studies and are cited in the text understate the contribution of a stable macroeconomy to a lower variability of performance at the level of the individual firm.

7. For references to implicit contract theory, see note 1 of Chapter 4.

8. See Ishikawa and Ueda (1984).

10. Is It Practical?

1. This case has been argued by Mitchell (1981, 1982).

References

Ackley, Gardner (1976): "Fiscal, Monetary, and Related Policies," in Patrick and Rosovsky, eds., *Asia's New Giant.*

Aoki, Masahiko, ed. (1984): *Economic Analysis of the Japanese Firm in Comparative Perspective.* Amsterdam: North Holland Publishing Co.

Ashley, W. J. (1903): *The Adjustment of Wages.* London: Longmans, Green.

Azariadis, Costas (1981): "Implicit Contracts and Related Topics: A Survey," in E. Hornstein et al., eds., *The Economics of the Labour Market.* London: HMSO.

Azariadis, Costas, and Joseph E. Stiglitz (1983): "Implicit Contracts and Fixed-Price Equilibria," *Quarterly Journal of Economics,* 98 (Supplement), 1–22.

Ball, R., and P. Brown (1967): "Some Preliminary Findings on the Association Between the Earnings of a Firm, Its Industry, and the Economy." Supplement to *Journal of Accounting Research*, Empirical Research in Accounting, Selected Studies, pp. 55–77.

Barkai, Haim (1977): *Growth Patterns of the Kibbutz Economy.* Amsterdam: North-Holland Publishing Co.

Bell, Daniel, and Irving Kristol, eds. (1981): *The Crisis in Economic Theory.* New York: Basic Books.

Berg, Norman, and Norman Fast (1975): "The Lincoln Electric Company." Cambridge: Harvard Business School Case Services.

Berliner, Joseph S. (1976): *The Innovation Decision in Soviet Industry.* Cambridge: MIT Press.

Bishop, Robert L. (1964): "The Theory of Monopolistic Competition after Thirty Years—The Impact on General Theory," *American Economic Review: Papers and Proceedings,* 54 (May), 33–43.

Carnegie, Andrew (1900): *The Gospel of Wealth and Other Timely Essays.* Cambridge: Harvard University Press reprint (1962).

Chamberlin, Edward M. (1933): *The Theory of Monopolistic Competition.* Cambridge: Harvard University Press, 1st ed. 1933, 8th ed. 1962.

Cheung, Steven N. S. (1969): *The Theory of Share Tenancy.* Chicago: University of Chicago Press.

Cohen, Jon, and Martin L. Weitzman (1975): "A Marxian Model of Enclosures," *Journal of Development Economics* (March).

Economic Report of the President (1983). Washington: U.S. Government Printing Office.

Foster, George (1978): *Financial Statement Analysis.* New York: Prentice-Hall.

Friedman, Milton (1968): "The Role of Monetary Policy," *American Economic Review,* 59 (March), 1–17.

Friedman, Milton and Rose (1979): *Free to Choose.* New York: Harcourt, Brace, Jovanovich.

Galenson, Walter (1976): "The Japanese Labor Market," in Patrick and Rosovsky, eds., *Asia's New Giant.*

References

Glazer, Nathan (1976): "Social and Cultural Factors in Japanese Economic Growth," in Patrick and Rosovsky, eds., *Asia's New Giant.*

Grossman, Sanford J. (1981): "An Introduction to the Theory of Rational Expectations Under Asymmetric Information," *Review of Economic Studies,* 48 (April), 541–549.

Hamermesh, Daniel S., and Albert Rees (1984): *The Economics of Work and Pay,* 3rd ed. New York: Harper and Row.

Hart, Oliver D. (1983): "Optimal Labour Contracts under Asymmetric Information: An Introduction," *Review of Economic Studies,* 50 (January), 3–35.

Hicks, John R. (1964): *The Theory of Wages,* 2nd ed. London: Macmillan.

———— (1974): *The Crisis in Keynesian Economics.* New York: Basic Books.

———— (1983): "The Keynes Centenary: A Skeptical Follower," *The Economist* (June 18), 17–19.

Ishikawa, Tsuneo, and Kazuo Ueda (1984): "The Bonus Payment System and Japanese Personal Savings," chapter 5 of Aoki, ed., *Economic Analysis of the Japanese Firm in a Comparative Perspective.*

Kaldor, Nicholas (1972): "The Irrelevance of Equilibrium Economics," *Economic Journal,* 82 (December).

Kaldor, Nicholas (1983): "Keynesian Economics After Fifty Years," in Trevithick and Worswick, eds., *Keynes and the Modern World.*

Kalecki, Michal (1943): "Political Aspects of Full Employment," *Political Quarterly,* 14 (January), 322–330.

Keynes, John Maynard (1921): *A Treatise on Probability.* London: Macmillan.

———— (1936): *The General Theory of Employment, Interest and Money.* Harcourt, Brace.

———— (1937): "The General Theory of Employment," *Quarterly Journal of Economics,* 51 (February), 209–223.

Keynes, Milo, ed. (1975): *Essays on John Maynard Keynes.* Cambridge: Cambridge University Press.

Knight, Frank H. (1921): *Risk, Uncertainty and Profit*. New York: Kelley Reprint of Economic Classics (1964).

———— (1923): "The Ethics of Competition." *Quarterly Journal of Economics*, 37 (August), 579–624.

Kornai, Janos (1980): *Economics of Shortage*. Amsterdam: North Holland Publishing Co.

———— (1983): "The Problem with Socialist Economies," *Forbes* (August 1), 64–67.

Lancaster, Kelvin J. (1979): *Variety, Equity, and Efficiency*. New York: Columbia University Press.

Latta, Geoffrey W. (1979), *Profit Sharing, Employee Stock Ownership, Savings, and Asset Formation Plans in the Western World*. Multinational Industrial Relations Series 5, University of Pennsylvania, Industrial Research Unit of the Wharton School.

Lekachman, Robert (1966): *The Age of Keynes*. New York: McGraw-Hill.

Lerner, Abba P. (1951): *Economics of Employment*. New York: McGraw-Hill.

Lewis, H. Gregg (1963): *Unionism and Relative Wages in the United States*. Chicago: University of Chicago Press.

Lief, Alfred (1958): *It Floats*. New York: Rhinehart.

Lincoln, Jonathan (1909): "The Sliding Scale of Wages in the Cotton Industry," *Quarterly Journal of Economics*, 23 (May), 450–469.

Lucas, Robert E. (1977): "Understanding Business Cycles," in K. Brunner and A. Meltzer, eds., *Stabilization of the Domestic and International Economy*. Carnegie-Rochester Series on Public Policy, vol. 5.

Lucas, Robert E., and Thomas Sargent (1978): "After Keynesian Macroeconomics," in *After the Phillips Curve: The Persistence of High Unemployment and High Inflation*. Boston: Federal Reserve Bank of Boston.

Luxemburg, Rosa (1913): *The Accumulation of Capital*. New York: Monthly Review Press (1968).

Marshall, Ray (1979): "Implications of Labor Market Theory for

Employment Policy," in G. I. Swanson and J. Michaelson, eds., *Manpower Research and Labor Economics.* Beverly Hills: Sage Publications.

Meade, James E. (1975): "The Keynesian Revolution," in Keynes, ed., *Essays on John Maynard Keynes.*

——— (1978): "The Meaning of 'Internal Balance'," *Economic Journal,* 88, 423–435.

——— (1979): "The Adjustment Process of Labour Co-Operatives with Constant Returns in Scale and Perfect Competition," *Economic Journal,* 89, 781–788.

——— (1982): *Stagflation. Vol. 1: Wage-Fixing.* London: Allen & Unwin.

Metzger, Bert L. (1978): *Profit Sharing in 38 Large Companies,* vols. 1 and 2. Evanston: Profit Sharing Research Foundation.

Mitchell, Daniel J. B. (1981): "Alternatives to Current Anti-Inflation Policy," in Mitchell, Bosworth, and Seidman, eds., *Controlling Inflation.* Washington: Center for Democratic Policy.

——— (1982): "Gain-Sharing: An Anti-Inflation Reform," *Challenge,* 25 (July-August), 18–25.

Munro, J. E. Crawford (1885): *Sliding Scales in the Iron Industry.* Manchester: Manchester Statistical Society.

Nakamura, Takafusa (1983): *Economic Growth in Postwar Japan.* New Haven: Yale University Press.

Nordhaus, William D. (1983): "Macroconfusion: The Dilemmas of Economic Policy," in J. Tobin, ed., *Macroeconomics, Prices, and Quantities.* Washington: The Brookings Institution.

Odaka, Kunio (1975): *Toward Industrial Democracy: Management and Workers in Modern Japan.* Cambridge: Harvard University Press.

OECD (1973): *Manpower Policy in Japan.* Paris: Organization for Economic Community and Development.

Okun, Arthur M. (1977): "The Great Stagflation Swamp," *Challenge* (November-December), 6–13.

Okuno, M. (1984): "Corporate Loyalty and Bonus Payments: An

Analysis of Work Incentives in Japan," in Aoki, ed., *Economic Analysis of the Japanese Firm in a Comparative Perspective.*

Patrick, Hugh, and Henry Rosovsky, eds. (1976): *Asia's New Giant.* Washington: The Brookings Institution.

Perloff, Jeffrey, and Michael Wachter (1979): "A Production Function Non-Accelerating Inflation Approach to Potential Output," in *Carnegie-Rochester Conference Series,* vol. 10, K. Brunner and A. Meltzer, eds., Amsterdam: North Holland Publishing Co.

Pigou, Arthur C. (1933): *Theory of Unemployment.* London: Macmillan.

———— (1937): "Real and Money Wage Rates in Relation to Unemployment," *Economic Journal,* 47 (September), 405.

Reynolds, Lloyd G. (1982): *Labor Economics and Labor Relations,* 8th ed. Homewood: Irwin.

Samuelson, Paul A. (1974): "Worldwide Stagflation," pp. 801–807 in vol. 4 of *The Collected Scientific Papers of Paul A. Samuelson.* Cambridge: MIT Press (1978).

Schloss, David F. (1892): *Methods of Industrial Remuneration.* London: Williams and Norgate.

Schumpeter, Joseph A. (1942): *Capitalism, Socialism and Democracy.* New York: Harper and Row.

Scitovsky, Tibor (1978): "Asymmetries in Economics," *Scottish Journal of Political Economy,* 25 (November), 227–237.

Shackle, G.L.S. (1949): *Expectation in Economics.* Cambridge: Cambridge University Press.

Smart, William (1894): *Miners' Wages and the Sliding Scale.* Glasgow: James Maclehose and Sons.

Solow, Robert M. (1975): "The Intelligent Citizen's Guide to Inflation," *The Public Interest,* 38 (Winter), 30–66.

———— (1979): "Alternative Approaches to Macroeconomic Theory: A Partial View," *Canadian Journal of Economics,* 12 (August), 339–354.

References

———— (1980): "On Theories of Unemployment," *American Economic Review*, 70 (March), 1–11.

Sraffa, Piero (1926): "The Laws of Returns under Competitive Conditions," *Economic Journal*, 36 (December), 535–550.

Taira, Koji (1970): *Economic Development and the Labor Market in Japan*. New York: Columbia University Press.

Thurow, Lester C. (1983): *Dangerous Currents*. New York: Random House.

Tinbergen, Jan (1969): "The Use of Models: Experience and Prospects," Nobel Memorial Prize Lecture, reprinted in *American Economic Review*, 71 (December 1981), 17–22.

Tobin, James (1947): "Money Wage Rates and Unemployment," in *The New Economics*, S. E. Harris, ed. New York: Knopf.

Tobin, James (1965): "On Improving the Economic Status of the Negro," *Daedalus*, 94 (Fall), 878–898.

———— (1980): "Are the New Classical Models Plausible Enough to Guide Policy?" *Journal of Money, Credit, and Banking*, 12 (November), 788–799.

———— (1983): "Macroeconomics Under Debate," Cowles Foundation Discussion Paper 669 (June).

Trevithick, James, and David Worswick, eds. (1983): *Keynes and the Modern World*. Cambridge: Cambridge University Press.

Vanek, Jaroslav (1970): *The General Theory of Labor Managed Market Economies*. Ithaca: Cornell University Press.

Wanniski, Jude (1975): "The Mundell-Laffer Hypothesis," *The Public Interest*, 39 (Spring), 31–52.

———— (1978): *The Way the World Works*. New York: Simon and Schuster.

Weitzman, Martin L. (1974): "Prices vs. Quantities," *Review of Economic Studies*, 41 (October), 477–491.

———— (1982): "Increasing Returns and the Foundations of Unemployment Theory," *Economic Journal*, 92 (December), 787–804.

References

———— (1983): "Some Macroeconomic Implications of Alternative Compensation Systems," *Economic Journal,* 93 (December).

Willes, Mark H. (1981): "'Rational Expectations' as a Counterrevolution," in Bell and Kristol, eds., *The Crisis in Economic Theory.*

Wright, Harrison M., ed. (1961): *The "New Imperialism": Analysis of Late Nineteenth-Century Expansion.* Boston: D. C. Heath.

Young, Allyn (1928): "Increasing Returns and Economic Progress," *Economic Journal,* 38 (December), 527–542.

Index